Troubled Water

Saints, Sinners, Truth and Lies about the Global Water Crisis

With essays from

Robert F. Kennedy Jr.
Vandana Shiva
Maude Barlow
Tony Clarke
Greenpeace
Oxfam
and more

ANITA RODDICK
with Brooke Shelby Biggs

Proceeds from this book are going towards supporting grassroots groups, non-governmental organizations and individuals who are indeed the saints on the issue of water.

If you would like to re-use or reproduce any part of the text of this work then go ahead – email me for permission on staff@anitaroddick.com and I'll send you the copy. In return I ask that you use it well, credit the authors of any material you use and donate what you feel to be a fair sum to an appropriate NGO.

Anita Roddick Books
An Imprint of Anita Roddick Publications, Ltd.
93 East Street
Chichester
West Sussex
UK PO19 1HA

www.AnitaRoddick.com

Published by Anita Roddick Books 2004

Conceived by: Dame Anita Roddick
Editor: Brooke Shelby Biggs
Design: Wheelhouse Creative, Ltd.
www.WheelhouseCreative.co.uk
Picture Research: Karen Weaver

A catalogue record for this book is available from the British Library.

ISBN: 0 954 3959 3X

Printed in the United Kingdom by Butler and Tanner, Frome.

Printed on ECF-rated, 100% recycled paper.

Distributed in the United Kingdom by Airlift Book Company, 8 The Arena, Mollison Avenue, Enfield, Middlesex, EN3 7NL

Distributed in North America by Chelsea Green Publishing, P.O. Box 428, 85 North Main Street, Suite 120, White River Junction, VT 05001

Acknowledgements

Anita Roddick and Brooke Shelby Biggs wish to thank: Medea Benjamin and Kevin Danaher for pointing us in the right direction when we were first wading into the subject; Satish Kumar for hosting the conference that first inspired this book; Wheelhouse Creative, whose creativity still astounds us; Michelle Williams of Book Production Consultants plc and David Holmes, without whom this book could not have been produced; Karen Bishop and Helen Cocker, the most organized people we know, whose tenacity ensures that everything actually happens; to the activists and grassroots organizers; and finally, and most importantly, to all the authors who contributed to this book - thank you for your wisdom, vision and generosity.

MILLION GALLONS OF WATER ARE NEEDED TO PRODUCE ONE DAY'S SUPPLY OF NEWSPRINT IN THE U.S

IT TAKES 20 GALLONS OF WATER TO RUN THE DISHWASHER

COST RATIO OF BOTTLED WATER TO NEW YORK CITY TAP WATER: 1,000 TO 1

PERCENTAGE OF AMERICANS WHO REGULARLY DRINK BOTTLED WATER 54

IF YOU LEAVE THE TAP ON WHEN YOU BRUSH YOUR TEETH, 4 TO 6 GALLONS OF WATER WILL GO DOWN THE DRAIN

A 10-MINUTE SHOWER USES 10 GALLONS OF WATER.

A TYPICAL BATH USES MORE THAN 40 GALLONS

A SINGLE TOILET FLUSH USES 3 TO 7 GALLONS OF WATER.

contents

Water is elemental, life-giving and sustaining. It is ours to drink, ours to play in, to grow with, to build on. Water is more fundamental than any other substance on Earth: You can live three weeks without food, but without water you'll be dead in three days.

01 Introduction

Anita Roddick

There is no more basic need than survival, and no substance on earth more crucial to survival than water. This makes it attractive to privatize and commodify, and one worth fighting and dying for. It is a capitalist's dream, and a warrior's cause.

But water cannot simply be a commodity to be exchanged and bartered by a few corporations, owned and controlled by big business. It is a human need and a right.

In the West I am seeing how prosperous agribusinesses have become addicted to expensive, outlandish solutions for turning deserts into farmland any place they can get their hands on. River systems are being diverted or choked off right under our noses, wilderness destroyed to keep crops growing where they do not belong (not to mention golf courses, racetracks and suburban lawns). Seemingly endless irrigation canals lose thousands of gallons of water to evaporation in a single hot and windy afternoon. Natural swamps are dying in the American South thanks to the cotton industry. Water used for the irrigation of these pesticide-laden crops has nowhere to drain, so it is customarily pumped into "evaporation ponds" – visibly foul, noxious soups of toxins rendering the soil beneath them lifeless and life-threatening.

The pump don't work 'cause the vandals took the handle.

Bob Dylan

What a dismal state of affairs.

I've done a lot of traveling in the Southern Hemisphere, as well – to places where they have no water and to places where they have too much. The people at these two extremes often have more in common than you'd think.

Physics dictates that water takes the path of least resistance, but for most people on this planet, the path to water is a bloody hard road. One billion people worldwide do not have any water within a 15-minute walk of their homes.

When the well is dry we know the value of water.

Benjamin Franklin

CHILDREN PLAY AT A BORE WELL PROVIDED BY OXFAM IN CAMBODIA.

In Africa, 40 billion working hours are lost each year because people, mainly women, have to spend them fetching and carrying water.

The average African family uses about 5 gallons (23 liters) of water a day. When you consider that the average American family uses more than 250 gallons (946 liters), it's just as well they don't have to walk to get it.

People say that there will be wars over water. Will be? There always have been. There are scads of references in the Bible to water. Back then, as now,

Fortunately, fighting back is the new politics of the 21st Century.

the power politics of the Middle East is still centered on water. We forget that the immediate cause of the Six Day War in 1967 between Israel and the Arab states was over access to water. Since seizing the West Bank, Israel has been using 79 percent of the water from the Mountain Aquifer and all of the water from the Jordan River basin. The crisis today is about land, yes, but also - and perhaps more so - about the water that flows under, into, and out of that land.

Wealth follows power, and power follows water. Robert F. Kennedy Jr. recently told me, "We are witnessing something unprecedented: Water no longer flows downhill. It flows toward money."

That fact is hardly lost on the multinationals. "Water is one of the great business opportunities," notes *Fortune* magazine. "It promises to be for the 21st Century what oil was for the 20th." Coca-Cola's 1993 annual report said, *"All of us in the Coca-Cola family wake up each morning knowing that every single one of the world's 5.6 billion people will get thirsty that day. If we make it impossible for these 5.6 billion people to escape Coca-Cola, then we assure our future success for many years to come. Doing anything else is not an option."* (Coca-Cola owns dozens of bottled water brands, including Dasani and Evian in the United States, Pump in Australia, and Malvern in the UK. Pepsi is a close competitor, but Nestlé beats both with 77 global brands.)

And maybe this is what the future will look like - depleted water supplies will have changed everything: fresh, naturally clean water will be so rare it will be guarded by armies. Ammunition for a

We are witnessing something unprecedented: Water no longer flows downhill. It flows toward money.

Robert F. Kennedy Jr.

toy water pistol is more expensive than platinum, riot police squads negotiate instead of firing water cannons (no bad thing). Imagine no more umbrellas! Naturally clean water is going the way of the dodo, and we need to do something about it now.

Fortunately, fighting back is the new politics of the 21st Century. Everywhere power is being dissolved down to the level of the community. In this grassroots global revolution, we find people are quietly getting on with changing the lives of their communities positively. And where people are finding creative technological solutions undreamed of by the Microsofts, Bayers and Exxons of this world.

These people know that freedom isn't just about the right to vote a dozen times during one's life, but the right to decide one's economic as well as political destiny. And that is precisely what economic globalization is stealing from people all over the world.

This book is a small effort to explore not just the problems of water worldwide, but to identify and celebrate some possible solutions.

Thirsty?

Anita Roddick

www.AnitaRoddick.com

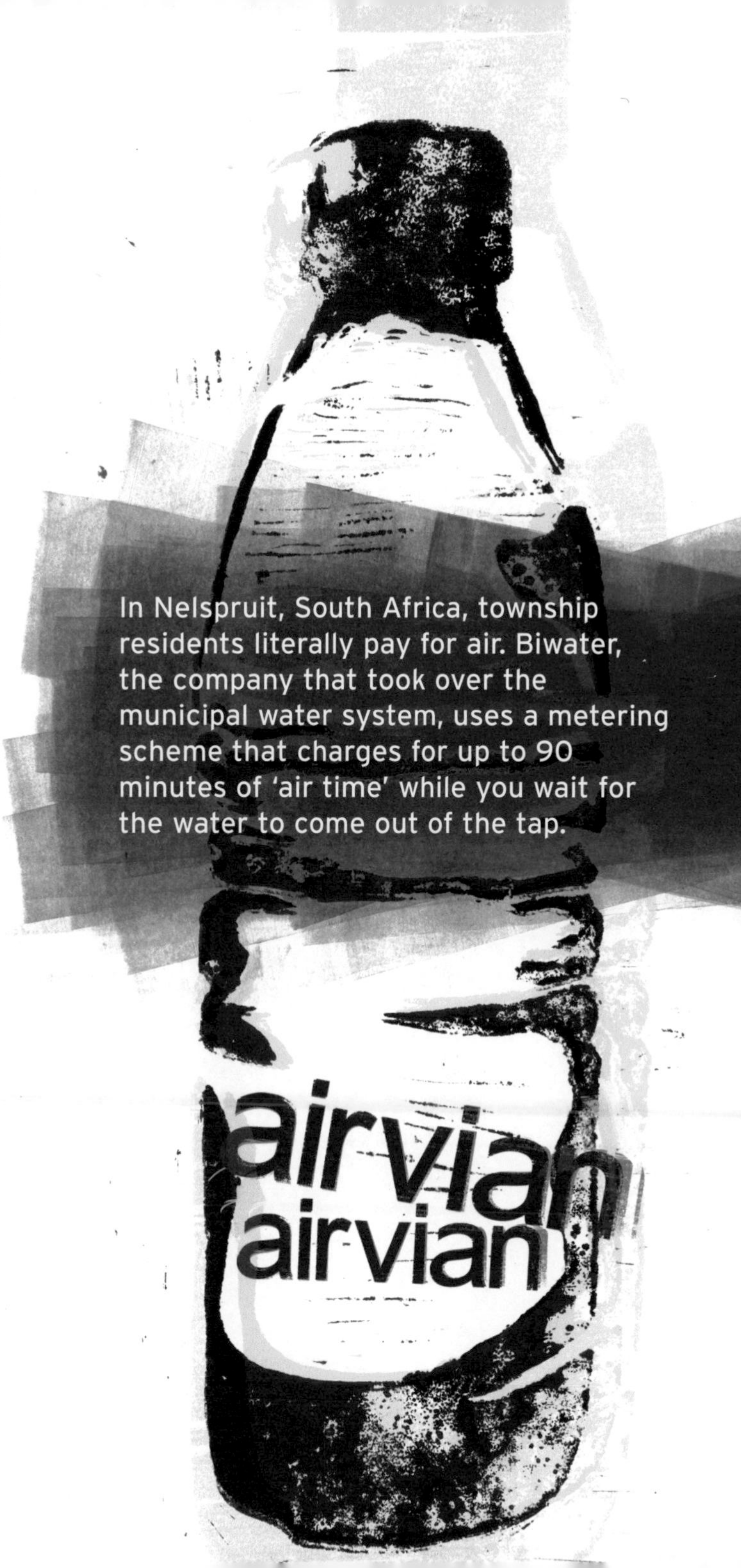

In Nelspruit, South Africa, township residents literally pay for air. Biwater, the company that took over the municipal water system, uses a metering scheme that charges for up to 90 minutes of 'air time' while you wait for the water to come out of the tap.

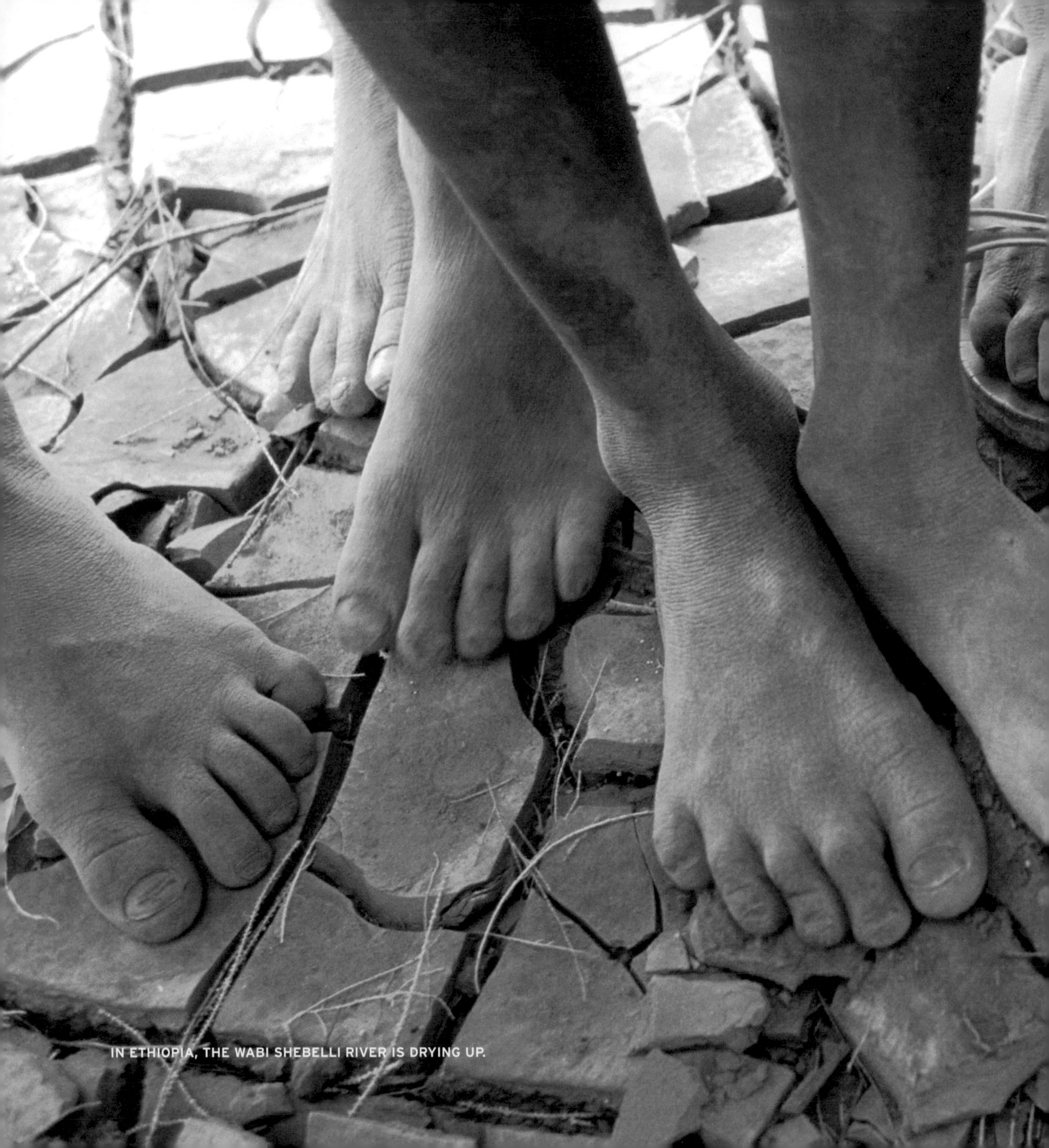

IN ETHIOPIA, THE WABI SHEBELLI RIVER IS DRYING UP.

One billion people worldwide do not have any water within a 15-minute walk of their homes.

WITHOUT WATER WE WOULD DIE WITHIN 3 DAYS

IN CASE OF
EMERGENCY
BREAK GLASS

Faced with the suddenly well-documented freshwater crisis, governments and international financial institutions are advocating the privatization and commodification of water.

02 The Lords of Water

Maude Barlow and Tony Clarke

Because the world is running out, freshwater has become the "Blue Gold" of the 21st century - a precious commodity that will determine the fate of nations and societies. Suddenly, the private sector has become intensely interested in the future of water and is moving in to take control of this finite and depleting resource. Competitive nation-states are abandoning natural resources protection and privatizing their ecological commons. Price water, they say in chorus; put it up for sale and let the market determine its future.

The agenda is clear: Water should be treated like any other tradable good, with its use determined by the principles of profit.

And so, a handful of transnational corporations, backed by the World Bank and the International Monetary Fund, are aggressively taking over the management of public water services in countries around the world, dramatically raising the price of water to local residents and profiting especially from the Third World's desperate search for solutions to its water crisis. Some are startlingly open: The decline in fresh water supplies and standards has created a wonderful venture opportunity for water corporations and their investors, they boast. The agenda is clear: Water should be treated like any other tradable good, with its use determined by the principles of profit.

There are 10 major corporate players now delivering freshwater services for profit. Between them, the three biggest - Suez and Vivendi Environment of France and RWE-AG of Germany - deliver water and wastewater services to almost 300 million customers in more than 100 countries, and are in a race - along with the others such as Bouygues SAUR, Thames Water (owned by RWE) and Bechtel-United Utilities - to expand to every corner of the globe. Their growth is exponential; a decade ago, they serviced around 51 million people in just 12 countries. And, although less than 10 percent of the world's water systems are currently under private control, at the rate they are expanding, the top three

IF THE WARS OF THIS CENTURY WERE FOUGHT OVER

OIL...

...THE WARS OF THE NEXT CENTURY WILL BE FOUGHT OVER

WATER

Ismail Serageldin World Bank vice president

alone will control more than 70 percent of the water systems in Europe and North America in a decade.

The revenue growth of the big three has kept pace. Vivendi earned just $5 billion a decade ago in its water-related revenues; by 2002 that had reached beyond $12 billion. RWE, which moved into the world market with its acquisition of Britain's Thames Water, increased its water revenue a whopping 9,786 percent in 10 years. All three are among the top 100 corporations in the world; together their annual revenue in 2001 was almost $160 billion and growing at 10 percent a year – outpacing the economies of many of the countries in which they operate. They also employ more staff than most governments: Vivendi Environment employs 295,000 worldwide; Suez employs 173,000.

The companies are creating sophisticated lobby groups to encourage the passage of legislation friendly to their interests. In France, the big two have long had close political ties with national and local governments. In Washington, they have secured beneficial tax law changes and are working to persuade Congress to pass laws that would force cash-trapped municipalities to consider privatization of their water systems in exchange for federal grants and loans.

The performance of these companies in Europe and the developing world has been well documented: huge profits, higher prices for water, cut-offs to customers who cannot pay, little transparency in their dealings, reduced water quality, bribery, and corruption. Not surprisingly, a huge international civil society movement is growing to wrest control of local water sources from the lords of water.

As the world begins to turn its attention to the growing water shortage crisis, it will have to deal head-on with the theft now taking place by these corporations. A water-secure future depends on creating a global water trust that must never be used to line the pockets of a greedy few.

Maude Barlow, chairman of the Council of Canadians, and Tony Clarke, director of the Polaris Institute, are the co-authors of ***Blue Gold, The Battle Against the Corporate Theft of the World's Water*****, published in 17 countries.**

WARNING
EVERY 8 SECONDS A CHILD DIES
FROM CONTAMINATED WATER

Please detach this part of your bill and send it along with payment in the envelope provided to:

A WATER COMPANY

A Water Company
HQ Water
Zambia Main Street
Lusaka
Zambia
Z100BT1

Mr A Customer
High Road
Lusaka
Zambia
Z200 BG2

Our Ref. 2548 8654 5351-95
Customer No. 2541865875-4

Total due

$ 250.00

...se refer to the reverse of this bill.

Please detach this part of your bill and send it along with payment in the envelope provided to:

ANOTHER WATER COMPANY

Another Water Company
HQ Water
New York City
NY 415 356
USA

Mr A Customer
Main Avenue
New York City
NY 212 324
USA

Our Ref. 3254 8543 5219-47
Customer No. 2549204875-1

Total due

$ 5.00

For details of alternative payment methods please refer to the reverse of this bill.

CITY DWELLERS IN THE THIRD WORLD MAY PAY UP TO 50 TIMES AS MUCH FOR WATER AS CITY DWELLERS IN EUROPE AND AMERICA

Before April 2000, few people outside of Bolivia had ever heard of Cochabamba, a city of 600,000, tucked away in the Andes. Today Cochabamba has become a powerful symbol in the fight for globalization with justice.

03 The Blue Revolution

Jim Shultz, The Democracy Center

Standing down soldiers, resisting a declaration of martial law, and rising up against a wave of economic theology, South America's poorest people evicted one of the world's wealthiest corporations and took back something simple and basic - their water.

In the 1980s and 1990s, the World Bank and International Monetary Fund made Bolivia a key testing ground for a set of economic policies imposed from above - a program dubbed by its critics as "neoliberalism." Under the threat of losing international loans, aid, and debt relief, Bolivia sold off its national airline, railroad, and electric company into private hands, often with disastrous results. In June 1997, World Bank officials told Bolivia's president that $600 million in international debt relief was dependent on Cochabamba privatizing its water system. In September 1999, in a closed-door process with just one bidder, Bolivian officials leased off Cochabamba's water until the year 2039 to a subsidiary of the California engineering giant, Bechtel.

More than 175 people were wounded, most victims of tear gas canisters or police beatings.

Just weeks after taking over the water, Bechtel's company hit local families with rate increases of up to 200 percent and sometimes higher. Workers living on the local minimum wage of $60 per month were told to pay as much as $15 just to keep the water running out of their tap. Tanya Paredes, a mother of four who supports her family knitting baby clothes, saw her water bill increased from $5 per month to nearly $20, a rise equal to what it costs her to feed her family for a week and a half. "What we pay for water comes out of what we have to pay for food, clothes and the other things we need to buy for our children," she said.

A new coalition of factory workers, irrigators and farmers, environmental groups and others was formed to challenge the privatization - the Coalition for the Defense of Water and Life, *La Coordinadora*. In January 2000, after the water company announced its huge rate increases, the *Coordinadora*

> Whiskey is for drinking;
> water is for fighting over.
>
> Mark Twain

DEMONSTRATORS PROTEST
AGAINST WATER RATE INCREASES.

organized a citywide general strike. For three days Cochabamba was shut down tight as a drum. Blockades closed down the two main highways leading in and out of town. The airport was closed. Roadblocks fashioned out of piles of rocks and tree branches cut off all traffic in the city. Thousands of Cochabambinos occupied the city's tree-lined, colonial central plaza. Under enormous public pressure, the government signed an agreement to review water rates.

Leaders of the protest were flown to a remote jail in Bolivia's jungle. Soldiers forced local television and radio stations off the air.

Then the government broke its word. With no change in rates forthcoming, the *Coordinadora* announced a new protest march to the city's main plaza in early February. The government declared the protest illegal and sent in 1,200 heavily armed police and soldiers to seize control of the city's center. Bechtel's contract would be protected with tear gas and bullets. More than 175 people were wounded, most victims of tear gas canisters or police beatings. The government lost all public legitimacy and finally announced a temporary rate rollback for six months.

As *Coordinadora* leaders began to examine the contract more closely, they decided that the real issue was not just rolling back rates but repealing the contract altogether and putting Cochabamba's water back under public control. In April, the *Coordinadora* announced what it called *La Ultima Batalla*, the Final Battle, a general strike and blockade of the highways that would not be lifted until the water contract was canceled and a new law enacted to guarantee water rights. After two days, local government officials finally agreed to a negotiation session moderated by Cochabamba's Catholic Archbishop. Police, under orders from the national government, burst into the meeting and put the *Coordinadora* leaders under arrest.

The next day Bolivia's president, Hugo Banzer, who had ruled over the nation during the 1970s as a dictator, imposed a state of martial law. Leaders of the protest were flown to a remote jail in Bolivia's jungle. Others went into hiding. Soldiers forced local television and radio stations off the air.

The public response was quick and furious. In my neighborhood, an old woman with a bent back laid out rocks in our street to block it. Young people, dubbed "the water warriors," headed downtown to challenge Banzer's troops. Women traveled door to door to collect rice and other food to cook for the people who remained camped in the plaza.

On Saturday afternoon a local television station captured footage of an army captain, Robinson Iriarte de La Fuente (a graduate of the United States Army's School of the Americas) disguised in plain clothes as he shot live rounds into a crowd of protesters. An unarmed 17-year-old boy, Victor Hugo Daza, was shot and killed with a bullet through the face. His friends carried his bloody body to the main plaza and held a wake.

Bechtel's officials fled the country, the water contract was canceled and a new, publicly controlled water company was installed.

While President Banzer's public relations staff told foreign reporters, falsely, that the Cochabamba protests were being orchestrated by "narcotraffickers," we at The Democracy Center were sending out reports directly from the scene via the Internet, accounts published in daily newspapers across the U.S. and Canada. Hundreds of people worldwide sent emails to the corporation's CEO demanding that the company leave. It was also becoming clear that the people of Cochabamba would not back down. Bechtel's officials fled the country, the water contract was canceled and a new, publicly controlled water company was installed. Cochabamba's water revolt became an international symbol of popular resistance to global economic rules imposed from above.

In November 2001, Bechtel filed a $25 million legal action against Bolivia in a secret trade court operated by the World Bank, the same institution that had forced the water privatization to begin with. In a process so secret that Bank officials won't reveal when hearings are held, who testifies, or what they say, Bechtel hopes to take from Bolivians an amount

Water that has been begged for does not quench the thirst.

Ugandan Proverb

equal to what it costs to hire 12,000 public school teachers. In August 2002, more than 300 citizen groups from 41 different countries filed an International Citizens Petition with the World Bank, demanding that the doors of its secret trade court be opened up to public scrutiny and participation.

"Many people say it is impossible to fight against the neoliberal model," says Leny Olivera, a 23-year-old university student involved in the protests. "But we showed that you can, not just in Bolivia but in the world. The humble people are the majority and are more powerful than multinational corporations."

Jim Shultz is the director of The Democracy Center and resides in Cochabamba, Bolivia.

Nothing on earth is so weak and yielding as water, but for breaking down the firm and strong, it has no equal.
Lao-Tsze

nrecht. El agua es un derecho humano fundamental. Water is a fundamental human right. L'eau, c'est un droit humain fondamental.
El agua es un derecho humano fundamental. Water is a fundamental human right. L'eau, c'est un droit humain fondamental. Wasser
gua es un derecho humano fundamental. Water is a fundamental human right. L'eau, c'est un droit humain fondamental. Wasser ist e
chenrecht. El agua es un derecho humano fundamental. Water is a fundamental human right. L'eau, c'est un droit humain fondament
ndamentales Menschenrecht. El agua es un derecho humano fundamental. Water is a fundamental human right. L'eau, c'est un droit h
El agua es un derecho humano fundamental. Water is a fundamental human right. L'eau, c'est un droit humain fondamental. Wasser
enrecht. El agua es un derecho humano fundamental. Water is a fundamental human right. L'eau, c'est un droit humain fondamental.
undamentales Menschenrecht. El agua es un derecho humano fundamental. Water is a fundamental human right. L'eau, c'est un droit
in fundamentales Menschenrecht. El agua es un derecho humano fundamental. Water is a fundamental human right. L'eau, c'est un d
nrecht. El agua es un derecho humano fundamental. Water is a fundamental human right. L'eau, c'est un droit humain fondamental.
es Menschenrecht. El agua es un derecho humano fundamental. Water is a fundamental human right. L'eau, c'est un droit humain fo
enschenrecht. El agua es un derecho humano fundamental. Water is a fundamental human right. L'eau, c'est un droit humain fondame
tales Menschenrecht. El agua es un derecho humano fundamental. Water is a fundamental human right. L'eau, c'est un droit humain
nrecht. El agua es un derecho humano fundamental. Water is a fundamental human right. L'eau, c'est un droit humain fondamental.
entales Menschenrecht. El agua es un derecho humano fundamental. Water is a fundamental human right. L'eau, c'est un droit humai
ht. El agua es un derecho humano fundamental. Water is a fundamental human right. L'eau, c'est un droit humain fondamental. Was
recht. El agua es un derecho humano fundamental. Water is a fundamental human right. L'eau, c'est un droit humain fondamental.
El agua es un derecho humano fundamental. Water is a fundamental human right. L'eau, c'est un droit humain fondamental. Wasser i
ht. El agua es un derecho humano fundamental. Water is a fundamental human right. L'eau, c'est un droit humain fondamental. Wass

OUR BODIES ARE 70% WATER

enrecht. El agua es un derecho humano fundamental. Water is a fundamental human right. L'eau, c'est un droit humain fondamental.
r ist ein fundamentales Menschenrecht. El agua es un derecho humano fundamental. Water is a fundamental human right. L'eau, c'es
entales Menschenrecht. El agua es un derecho humano fundamental. Water is a fundamental human right. L'eau, c'est un droit humai
El agua es un derecho humano fundamental. Water is a fundamental human right. L'eau, c'est un droit humain fondamental. Wasser
ein fundamentales Menschenrecht. El agua es un derecho humano fundamental. Water is a fundamental human right. L'eau, c'est un d
enschenrecht. El agua es un derecho humano fundamental. Water is a fundamental human right. L'eau, c'est un droit humain fondam
derecho humano fundamental. Water is a fundamental human right. L'eau, c'est un droit humain fondamental. Wasser ist ein fundame
ntales Menschenrecht. El agua es un derecho humano fundamental. Water is a fundamental human right. L'eau, c'est un droit humai
t. El agua es un derecho humano fundamental. Water is a fundamental human right. L'eau, c'est un droit humain fondamental. Wasse
Menschenrecht. El agua es un derecho humano fundamental. Water is a fundamental human right. L'eau, c'est un droit humain fond
ht. El agua es un derecho humano fundamental. Water is a fundamental human right. L'eau, c'est un droit humain fondamental. Was
s un derecho humano fundamental. Water is a fundamental human right. L'eau, c'est un droit humain fondamental. Wasser ist ein fu
echt. El agua es un derecho humano fundamental. Water is a fundamental human right. L'eau, c'est un droit humain fondamental. Wa
El agua es un derecho humano fundamental. Water is a fundamental human right. L'eau, c'est un droit humain fondamental. Wasser i
les Menschenrecht. El agua es un derecho humano fundamental. Water is a fundamental human right. L'eau, c'est un droit humain fo
echt. El agua es un derecho humano fundamental. Water is a fundamental human right. L'eau, c'est un droit humain fondamental. Wa
El agua es un derecho humano fundamental. Water is a fundamental human right. L'eau, c'est un droit humain fondamental. Wasser i
mentales Menschenrecht. El agua es un derecho humano fundamental. Water is a fundamental human right. L'eau, c'est un droit hum
l agua es un derecho humano fundamental. Water is a fundamental human right. L'eau, c'est un droit humain fondamental. Wasser is
recht. El agua es un derecho humano fundamental. Water is a fundamental human right. L'eau, c'est un droit humain fondamental. W
ntales Menschenrecht. El agua es un derecho humano fundamental. Water is a fundamental human right. L'eau, c'est un droit humain
cht. El agua es un derecho humano fundamental. Water is a fundamental human right. L'eau, c'est un droit humain fondamental. Was
undamentales Menschenrecht. El agua es un derecho humano fundamental. Water is a fundamental human right. L'eau, c'est un droit
t. El agua es un derecho humano fundamental. Water is a fundamental human right. L'eau, c'est un droit humain fondamental. Wasse
ntales Menschenrecht. El agua es un derecho humano fundamental. Water is a fundamental human right. L'eau, c'est un droit humain
echt. El agua es un derecho humano fundamental. Water is a fundamental human right. L'eau, c'est un droit humain fondamental. Wa
Menschenrecht. El agua es un derecho humano fundamental. Water is a fundamental human right. L'eau, c'est un droit humain fond

fundamentales Menschenrecht. El agua es un derecho humano fundamental. Water is a fundamental human right. L'eau, c'est un dro
mentales Menschenrecht. El agua es un derecho humano fundamental. Water is a fundamental human right. L'eau, c'est un droit hum
ales Menschenrecht. El agua es un derecho humano fundamental. Water is a fundamental human right. L'eau, c'est un droit humain f
ein fundamentales Menschenrecht. El agua es un derecho humano fundamental. Water is a fundamental human right. L'eau, c'est un
mental. Wasser ist ein fundamentales Menschenrecht. El agua es un derecho humano fundamental. Water is a fundamental human rig
mentales Menschenrecht. El agua es un derecho humano fundamental. Water is a fundamental human right. L'eau, c'est un droit hum
n fundamentales Menschenrecht. El agua es un derecho humano fundamental. Water is a fundamental human right. L'eau, c'est un dr
lamental. Wasser ist ein fundamentales Menschenrecht. El agua es un derecho humano fundamental. Water is a fundamental human r
'ondamental. Wasser ist ein fundamentales Menschenrecht. El agua es un derecho humano fundamental. Water is a fundamental huma
fundamentales Menschenrecht. El agua es un [illegible] ter is a fundamental human right. L'eau, c'est un dro
'asser ist ein fundamentales Menschenrecht [illegible] Water is a fundamental human right. L'eau,
ist ein fundamentales Menschenrecht [illegible] a fundamental human right. L'eau, c'est
Wasser ist ein fundamentales M [illegible] ter is a fundamental human right. L'e
fundamentales Menschenrecht [illegible] tal human right. L'eau, c'est un dro
l. Wasser ist ein fundamen [illegible] a fundamental human right. L'
ndamentales Menschenr [illegible] right. L'eau, c'est un droit h
fundamentales Mensch [illegible] an right. L'eau, c'est un dro
nentales Menschenre [illegible] L'eau, c'est un droit huma
ndamentales Mensch [illegible] t. L'eau, c'est un droit h
'asser ist [illegible] right. L'eau,
lamentale [illegible] roit hu

OUR PLANET IS 70% WATER

fundam [illegible] un dro
l. Wasser [illegible] ght. L'e
undamentales [illegible] L'eau, c'est un droit
in fundamentales [illegible] ht. L'eau, c'est un dr
umain fondamen [illegible] Vater is a fundamenta
tal. Wasser ist ei [illegible] mental human right. I
amentales Mensc [illegible] au, c'est un droit hun
fondamental. Wa [illegible] is a fundamental hum
r ist ein fundame [illegible] uman right. L'eau, c'es
chenrecht. El agua [illegible] roit humain fondamenta
al. Wasser ist ein fu [illegible] mental human right. L
damentales Mensche [illegible] L'eau, c'est un droit hu
sser ist ein fundamen [illegible] ntal human right. L'eau, c
ndamentales Menschen [illegible] right. L'eau, c'est un droit
Menschenrecht. El agua [illegible] c'est un droit humain fonda
fundamentales Menschenrec [illegible] nan right. L'eau, c'est un droit
mentales Menschenrecht. El ag [illegible] right. L'eau, c'est un droit hum
Wasser ist ein fundamentales Me [illegible] is a fundamental human right. L'eau
'undamentales Menschenrecht. El agu [illegible] mental human right. L'eau, c'est un droit
mentales Menschenrecht. El agua es un de [illegible] amental human right. L'eau, c'est un droit hum
ental. Wasser ist ein fundamentales Menschenre [illegible] o fundamental. Water is a fundamental human right
nentales Menschenrecht. El agua es un derecho humano fundamental. Water is a fundamental human right. L'eau, c'est un droit huma
fundamentales Menschenrecht. El agua es un derecho humano fundamental. Water is a fundamental human right. L'eau, c'est un dro
al. Wasser ist ein fundamentales Menschenrecht. El agua es un derecho humano fundamental. Water is a fundamental human right. L
ndamentales Menschenrecht. El agua es un derecho humano fundamental. Water is a fundamental [illegible] eau, c'est un droit
damental. Wa [illegible] damental human

WATER IS A FUNDAMENTAL HUMAN RIGHT

damentales [illegible] est un droit hu
al. Wasser ist [illegible] al human right. L
fundamentales Menschenrecht. El agua es un derecho humano fundamental. Water is a fundamental human right. L'eau, c'est un droi
sser ist ein fundamentales Menschenrecht. El agua es un derecho humano fundamental. Water is a fundamental human right. L'eau, c'

A leaky faucet that loses a drop per second loses 16 bathtubs full a month, and 10,000 liters a year.

The average human should consume 2.5 liters of water a day. You'll pee 1.5 liters of it out, on average. If you cry, that's another 1ml. You may sweat from 1 to 3 liters a day.

The Aral Sea used to be the fourth largest lake on Earth. Because of water diversion for cotton crops, the lake could disappear by the year 2015. The dry lake bed has been poisoned by pesticides, and the remaining water is too saline to be used for anything. It doesn't even contain enough life to support the fishing industry – **once a thriving business along the Aral shore.**

The cure for anything is saltwater - sweat, tears, or the sea.

Tagore

04 Don't Buy the Lie: Myths of Privatization

Vandana Shiva

Privatization is necessary because society and governments do not have the capital to invest in water schemes.

Water corporations do not bring investment. They use World Bank/IMF loans that have water privatization as a condition built into them. The investment is public, the profits are private. The same mechanisms and policies that privatize water also impoverish municipalities, and local governments by reducing tax collections and revenue generation at local and regional level.

Water must be priced and made a marketable commodity because water available for free has led to overexploitation. Commodification will lead to conservation.

The Reality:

The water crisis results from an erroneous equation of value with monetary price. However, resources can often have very high value while having no price. Sacred sites like forests and rivers are examples of resources that have very high value but no price. Oceans, rivers, and other bodies of water have played important roles as metaphors for our relationship to the planet. Diverse cultures have different value systems through which the ethical, ecological, and economic behavior of society is guided and shaped. Similarly, the idea that life is sacred puts a high value on living systems and prevents their commodification.

Conservation is based on sacred values and ecological values. Sacred waters have no price, they cannot be commodified. Market value destroys spiritual and ecological values.

Markets create incentives for overexploitation, not for conservation or equitable distribution.

Water privatization is necessary to make water supply more efficient and reliable, and to increase access to clean water.

The Reality:

Privatization has reduced water access by increasing water costs. Once the water giants enter the picture, water prices go up. In Sibic Bay, the Philippines, Biwater increased water rates by 400 percent. In France, customer fees increased 150 percent but water quality deteriorated; a French government report revealed that more than 5.2 million people received "bacterially unacceptable water." In England, water rates increased by 450 percent, company profits soared by 692 percent, and CEO salaries increased by an astonishing 708 percent. Meanwhile, service disconnection increased by 50 percent, dysentery increased six-fold, and the British Medical Association condemned water privatization for its health effects.

In 1998, shortly after Sydney's water was taken over by Suez Lyonnaise des Eaux, it was contaminated with high levels of giardia and cryptosporidium. After water testing had been privatized by A&L Labs, in Walkerton, Ontario, seven people, including a baby, died as a result of E. coli. The company treated the test results as "confidential intellectual property" and refused to make them public. In Argentina, when a Suez Lyonnaise des Eaux subsidiary purchased the state-run water company Obras Sanitarias de la Nacion, water rates doubled but water quality deteriorated. The company was forced to leave the country when residents refused to pay their bills.

A BOY CARRIES WATER OVER
AN OPEN DITCH IN GHANA.

Water privatization will reduce the power of government and hence increase the role of citizens, thus enhancing democracy.

Water privatization is taking place through private-public partnerships between large corrupt corporations and corrupt government officials by circumventing all checks and balances of public participation, public planning, and public transparency. Private-public partnerships assume the only private is corporations, and the only public is centralized governments.

Privatization allows centralized governments to usurp the rights of communities and local authorities, lay claim to the water commons and sell them off to private companies which then sell the water back to those to whom it originally belonged. Governments start to operate on the eminent domain principle rather than the public trust doctrine, thus undermining and subverting democracy.

Privatization establishes property rights to water which gives water value and helps regulate water use.

Water is a commons, not private property. More than any other resource, water needs to remain a common good and requires community management. In fact, in most societies, private ownership of water has been prohibited. Ancient texts such as the *Institute of Justinian* show that water and other natural sources are public goods: "By the law of nature these things are common to mankind – the air, running water, the sea, and consequently the shore of the sea."

In countries like India, space, air, water, and energy have traditionally been viewed as being outside the realm of property relations. In Islamic traditions, the Sharia, which originally connoted the "path to water," provides the ultimate basis for the right to water.

Private property creates regulation by the market and creates the cowboy economy of "might is right." This leads to environmental and social deregulation, encouraging non-sustainable use and unjust distribution.

A GUARD AT THE GATE NEAR A
CHINESE DAM PROJECT SITE.

GIRLS FETCH WATER FROM A BORE WELL IN THE ARAL SEA REGION.

Water is not a human right, it is merely a human need.

Water has traditionally been treated as a natural right – a right arising out of nature, historic conditions, basic needs, or notions of justice. Water rights as natural rights do not originate with the state; they evolve out of a given ecological context of human existence.

As natural rights, water rights are usufructuary rights; water can be used but not owned. People have a right to life and therefore to the resources that sustain it, including water.

That is why governments and corporations cannot alienate people of their water rights. Water rights come from nature and creation. They flow from the laws of nature, not from the rules of the market.

Vandana Shiva, author of *Water Wars* and other seminal books, is the director of The Research Foundation for Science, Technology and Natural Resource Policy, and ecology adviser to the Third World Network.

Bangladesh has endured flood, famine and disease. Now it faces the largest mass poisoning in world history - from arsenic. As many as 80 million people may be affected, according to the World Health Organization.

05 Don't Drink the Water

Bob Forsberg and Sakil Faizullah

One expert says the situation makes the Chernobyl disaster "look like a Sunday school panic." But this tragedy is neither an act of terrorism nor a disastrous industrial accident. It is the result of an initiative to provide Bangladeshis with fresh water that went terribly wrong.

The country has one of the highest rates of waterborne diseases in the world. To combat this, in the early 1990s the government told people to stop drinking dirty surface water and instead drink cleaner groundwater. But it did not know then that much of the underground supplies contain levels of naturally occurring arsenic five times higher than the maximum recommended by the United Nations.

Arsenic affects the skin, causing melanosis, keratosis, spotting and scaling, warts and ulcerations, and can eventually lead to gangrene and skin cancer. It attacks most of the body's organs and there is increasing evidence that it causes a host of internal cancers and other chronic illnesses.

At present, poor sanitation kills more Bangladeshis than arsenicosis, but because the illness can take years to diagnose, doctors warn that in 10 years it could reach epidemic proportions, perhaps more urgent and dire even than the AIDS crisis in Africa.

In the village of Dalipara, 10 miles north of Chittagong, housewife and mother Laila Begum extracts groundwater using a pump. Until recently, she drank it regularly. But she stopped when a series of brown lumps started appearing on her skin - the first symptoms of arsenic poisoning.

"Ten years ago we were encouraged by the government to use groundwater because they said it was far cleaner than surface water," she says. "They even dug wells and provided pumps for us to use. At that time, no one knew of the dangers of arsenic poisoning. It was only when my skin started to go black and blotches appeared on my face that I went to see a doctor. He told me I had arsenicosis, which can kill me."

Laila and her young family now drink water from a nearby pond, risking cholera or worse. But at least it

WOMEN PUMP WATER FROM A WELL IN
A FLOODED NEIGHBORHOOD IN BANGLADESH.

is free of arsenic. She is weak from the poisoning but still has to work to look after her family.

In London, legal proceedings have begun in the High Court to decide whether a British organization was negligent in failing to detect it. The British Geological Survey, which conducted research on behalf of the Bangladesh government in 1992, is accused of not testing for arsenic and giving the groundwater a clean bill of health, even in places where arsenic was present at as much as 50 times the United Nations maximum. In its own defense, the BGS argues that, at the time of its report, little was known about the geological origins of arsenic poisoning.

Meanwhile, aid agencies and non-governmental organizations battle to give villages clean water. Many run arsenic mitigation programs, most of which involve various types of filters or harvesting rainwater. Hand pumps are painted red or green to show whether the water is contaminated, and only to be used for laundry and bathing, or if it is safe for cooking and drinking.

This essay was written by Bob Forsberg based on a report by Sakil Faizullah which aired on Radio Netherlands.

WHERE DOES WATER COME FROM?

Water is a closed system: All of the water that exists on earth today existed when the planet was first formed. The water in a dinosaur's drinking hole 250 million years ago may be the same water in your afternoon tea tomorrow. The river water polluted by toxic runoff may be in a baby's formula in 10 years.

condensation
precipitation
evaporation
collection

A POLLUTED RIVER RUNS THROUGH
A KUALA LUMPUR SLUM, MALAYSIA.

The sewer is the conscience of the city.
Victor Hugo

TROPIC OF CANCER
(23.27;)
EQUATOR
TROPIC OF CAPRICORN
(23.27;)

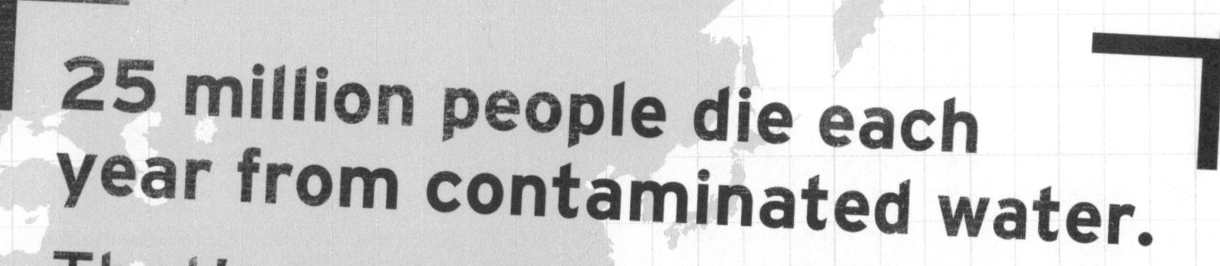

TROPIC OF CANCER

EQUATOR

TROPIC OF CAPRICORN

In India, communities near Coca-Cola bottling plants are finding their wells drying up. For some, a Coke is easier to come by than a glass of water.

06 Coca-Colanization

Amit Srivastava, India Resource Center

The Indian parliament banned the sale of Coke and Pepsi products in its cafeteria after tests in September 2003 found high concentrations of pesticides and insecticides - including lindane, DDT, malathion, and chlorpyrifos - in their sodas sold in India. Some samples tested showed the presence of these toxins to be more than 30 times the standard allowed by the European Union. This, however, is simply the latest in a series of offenses the cola giants have committed against the people of India. Both, for example, were slapped for painting unapproved advertising billboards, graffiti-style, on rockfaces in the Himalayas. The Indian Supreme Court called the companies "vandals" for defacing priceless scenery and fined them both.

The water Coca-Cola uses in a day would satisfy 20,000 Indian people.

Coca-Cola's offenses make a perfect example of how rural communities in developing nations are becoming pawns in a power grab by the World Trade Organization and multinational corporations which have their eyes on the ultimate prize: water. They seem to have no shame.

Communities in and around Coca-Cola's bottling operations are facing severe shortages of water because the company is sucking huge amounts of water from the common groundwater source for its operations. To add insult to injury, the scarce water that remains has been polluted by the bottling plants or contaminated by minerals sloughing from the walls of the overtapped aquifer. Villagers who use the water say it smells and tastes rank, and makes them sick to their stomachs and causes rashes to break out on their skin. The medical officer of the Public Health Center in one of the villages warned people not to drink the water from the three wells near the Coca-Cola plant due to contamination.

In a gesture of "goodwill" (or an admission of guilt), Coca-Cola now proudly sends water tankers into the communities from which it stole the water to begin with. And the primary raw material for all of Coca-Cola's products - water - is essentially free for the

company to exploit. In Kerala, the water Coca-Cola uses in a single day would satisfy the needs of 20,000 Indian people. But for communities near Coca-Cola bottling plants, the wells don't provide enough water of even the most basic quality to satisfy anyone at all. At least five communities across India located next to Coca-Cola facilities are facing similar problems, and the number of families affected, mostly the rural poor, runs into the thousands.

Worse still, Coca-Cola - in another "goodwill gesture" - briefly tried to give away the toxic sludge from its plant in Kerala to farmers for free ... as fertilizer. Tests commissioned by BBC on samples of the gunk found high levels of lead and cadmium.

Coca-Cola characterizes community organizers and village protestors as a "handful of extremists," and claims the water shortages in the communities are drought-related. Yet thousands of people continue to protest Coke facilities all across India.

Now Coca-Cola and its agents (including local police) are increasingly using force to deal with protests. On Sept. 11, 2003, armed security forces violently attacked a peaceful demonstration of more than a thousand community members in Mehdiganj, Uttar Pradesh, resulting in grave injuries to some protestors. Coca-Cola has claimed that the protestors were rioting and trespassing. On Aug. 30, 2003, this time in Kerala, 13 activists were arrested during a peaceful demonstration and a leader of the movement was severely beaten by the police.

Thousands of people continue to protest Coke facilities all across India.

Such blatant abuses by a large multinational like Coca-Cola highlight the problems of economic globalization. Communities no longer have any control over their natural resources or even development policies that directly affect their lives. The battle to hold Coca-Cola accountable is far from over. The struggle in Kerala has been growing and there has been a constant vigil, 24 hours a day, seven days a week, in front of Coca-Cola's factory since April 22, 2002. Similarly, communities in the Indian states of Maharashtra, Uttar Pradesh, Rajasthan, and Tamil Nadu are beginning to actively assert their rights as a community to the groundwater.

And sometimes, they win. In Kerala, the panchayat (local government) has canceled the license of Coca-Cola to operate and the high court in Kerala ruled in December 2003 that Coca-Cola has to find other sources of water for its bottling facility.

Amit Srivastava coordinates the India Resource Center, a project of Global Resistance.

WATER IS
THE ONLY
DRINK FOR A
WISE MAN.

Henry David Thoreau

1.4 billion

The estimated number of people worldwide who **lack access** to **clean drinking water.**

2.4 billion

The estimated number of people worldwide who lack access to **sanitation.** Most are in Africa and Asia.

40%

The **increase** in **global water use** expected by 2020.

$30 billion

The projected cost per year of bringing poor people **universal access** to water by 2015.

(Source: United Nations Environment Programme, GEO-Global Environment Outlook 3, Past, Present and Future Perspectives)

10

THAILAND'S PUBLIC HEALTH MINISTRY TELLS RAIN COLLECTORS TO **WAIT AN HOUR** AFTER A SHOWER STARTS BECAUSE THE RAIN IN INDUSTRIAL AREAS IS AS **ACID AS TOMATO JUICE.**

Water is sometimes sharp and sometimes strong, sometimes acid and sometimes bitter, sometimes sweet and sometimes thick or thin, sometimes it is seen bringing hurt or pestilence, sometimes health giving, sometimes poisonous. It suffers change into as many natures as are the different places through which it passes. And as the mirror changes with the color of its subject, so it alters with the nature of the place, becoming noisome, laxative, astringent, sulfurous, salty, incarnadined, mournful, raging, angry, red, yellow, green, black, blue, greasy, fat, or slim. Sometimes it starts a conflagration, sometimes it extinguishes one; is warm and is cold, carries away or sets down, hollows out or builds up, tears or establishes, fills or empties, raises itself or burrows down, speeds or is still; is the cause at times of life or death, or increase or privation, nourishes at times and at others does the contrary; at times has a tang, at times is without savor, sometimes submerging the valleys with great floods. In time and with water, everything changes.

Leonardo da Vinci

It's among the fastest-growing and least-regulated industries in the world. Now some of the largest beverage companies in the world are getting into the bottled water act, a $46 billion industry.

07 Evian Backward is Naïve

Maude Barlow and Tony Clarke

In the 1970s, the annual volume of water bottled and traded around the world was around 1 billion liters. But, by 2000, annual sales in bottled water had skyrocketed to 84 billion liters, one quarter of which was traded and consumed outside its country of origin. What's more, bottled water is one of the biggest scams in our daily lives, priced at a minimum of 1,100 times what the same amount of water taken from the tap would cost on average.

Nestlé is the world market leader in bottled water, with no fewer than 77 brands, including Perrier, Vittel, and San Pellegrino. As a past chairman of Perrier put it: "It struck me ... that all you had to do is take the water out of the ground and then sell it for more than the price of wine, milk, or for that matter, oil."

While bottled water may have started out as a pampered Western consumer affectation, Nestlé has found a growing market niche for bottled water in non-industrialized countries where safe tap water is rare or nonexistent. In many developing countries, its main product line is Nestlé Pure Life, a low-cost purified tap water with added minerals, which is marketed all over the world on a slogan of "basic wholesomeness."

"It struck me ... that all you had to do is take the water out of the ground and then sell it for more than the price of wine, milk, or for that matter, oil."

Perrier executive

In 2000, worldwide sales in bottled water were estimated to be around $22 billion. By 2003, the bottled water industry sales were pegged at $46 billion. Regardless of which figures are used as the benchmark, the bottled water industry has been growing at an astounding rate. Besides Nestlé, other giants of the global food and beverage industry have also become purveyors of bottled water, including Coca-Cola, PepsiCo, Procter & Gamble and Danone. With the entry of the big soft drink giants, market growth has rapidly accelerated. PepsiCo is currently leading the way with its Aquafina line, followed closely by Coca-Cola's Dasani in North America and

CHILDREN SCOUR RECYCLING MOUNDS IN THE PHILIPPINES.

Bon Aqua internationally. Both pop kings take their water from the tap and add minerals before selling it as bottled water.

Bottled water is not always safer than tap water, and some is less so.

Yet in contrast to the market image of "pure spring water" that is projected by the industry, bottled water is not always safer than tap water and some is less so. That was the conclusion of a 1999 study by the U.S.-based Natural Resources Defense Council (NRDC), which found that one-third of the 103 brands of bottled water it studied contained detectable levels of contamination, including traces of arsenic and E. coli. One-quarter of all bottled water is actually taken from the tap, though it is further processed and purified to some degree, according to the NRDC study. In many countries, bottled water itself is subject to less rigorous testing and lower purity standards than tap water. "One brand of 'spring water,'" reported the NRDC, "... actually came from a well in an industrial facility's parking lot, near a hazardous waste dump, and periodically was contaminated with industrial chemicals at levels above FDA standards."

The marketing hype about bottled water being more environmentally friendly and healthier than tap water is also misleading. In terms of nutritional value, according to the United Nations Food and Agricultural Organization (FAO), bottled water is no better than tap water. The idea that bottled "spring" or "natural" water contains near-magical qualities and great nutritive value is "false," according to a 1997 FAO study called "Human Nutrition in the Developing World": "Bottled water may contain small amounts of minerals such as calcium, magnesium, and fluoride, but so does tap water from many municipal water supplies." The FAO report also cites a study "comparing popular brands of bottled water [which] showed that they were in no way superior to New York tap water."

All bottled water sold in North America comes in plastic bottles which add to environmental concerns. A study released by the World Wildlife Fund (WWF) in May 2001 shows that the bottled water industry uses 1.5 million tons of plastic every year, and when plastic bottles are being manufactured or disposed of, they release toxic chemicals into the atmosphere. Furthermore, since a quarter of all bottled water produced is for export markets and transportation fuel results in carbon dioxide emissions, the WWF report contends that the transportation of bottled water is a contributing factor to the problem of global warming.

"One brand of 'spring water' ... actually came from a well in an industrial facility's parking lot near a hazardous waste dump."

Worse still, the relentless search for secure water supplies to feed the insatiable appetites of the water-bottling corporations is having damaging effects. In rural communities throughout much of the world (and several suburban communities in the United States and Canada), the industry has been buying up land to access wells and then moving on when the wells are depleted. In Uruguay and other parts of Latin America, foreign-based water corporations have been buying up vast wilderness tracts and even whole water systems to hold for future development. In some cases, these companies end up draining the aquifer that serves the entire area, not just the water on or directly under their land tracts.

Claiming private property rights, bottled water corporations generally pay no fee for the water they remove from lakes, rivers, and streams. In Canada, for example, where the amount of water extracted by the bottling industry has grown by 50 percent in the past decade, bottlers have a legal right to take about 30 billion liters a year – approximately 1,000 liters for every person in the country. Close to half of all this bottled water is exported to the United States. Yet unlike the oil industry, which pays royalties, and the timber industry, which pays stumpage fees to the government, the water-bottling business is not required to pay fees for the extraction of water in most Canadian jurisdictions.

The global gaps between rich and poor are also dramatically mirrored in the marketing strategies of the bottled water corporations. In its 1999 study, the NRDC reported that some people actually pay as much as 10,000 times more per gallon of bottled water than they do for tap water in their

communities. For the same price as one bottle of this "boutique" consumer item, says the American Water Works Association, one thousand gallons of tap water could be delivered to a person's home. Ironically, the same industry that contributes to the destruction of public water sources - in order to provide "pure" water to the world's elite in plastic bottles - is peddling its product as being environmentally friendly and part of a healthy lifestyle.

Tony Clarke, director of the Polaris Institute, and Maude Barlow, chairman of the Council of Canadians, are co-authors of *Blue Gold: The Battle Against the Corporate Theft of the World's Water*, now published in 17 countries

What can we do?

Bottled water should not be considered a sustainable alternative to tap water. It is not exempt from periodic contamination and is less energy-efficient than tap water. However not all countries have the benefit of clean tap water. Clean water is a basic right. Protecting our rivers, streams and wetlands will help ensure that tap water remains a public service which delivers good quality drinking water for everyone at a fair price.

As a consumer, make responsible choices and do not forget the 3 Rs:

1 Reduce your consumption

2 Reuse your water bottles

3 Recycle your bottles after you are finished with them.

UNESCO

WESTERN EUROPE: 85
46%

NORTH AMERICA: 35
20%

PACIFIC: 19
11%

EASTERN EUROPE: 15
8%

LATIN AMERICA: 12
7%

NORTH AFRICA AND THE NEAR EAST: 10
6%

ASIA: 3
2%

AFRICA: 2
0%

WORLD BOTTLED WATER CONSUMPTION

IN LITERS/YEAR/PERSON AND IN %

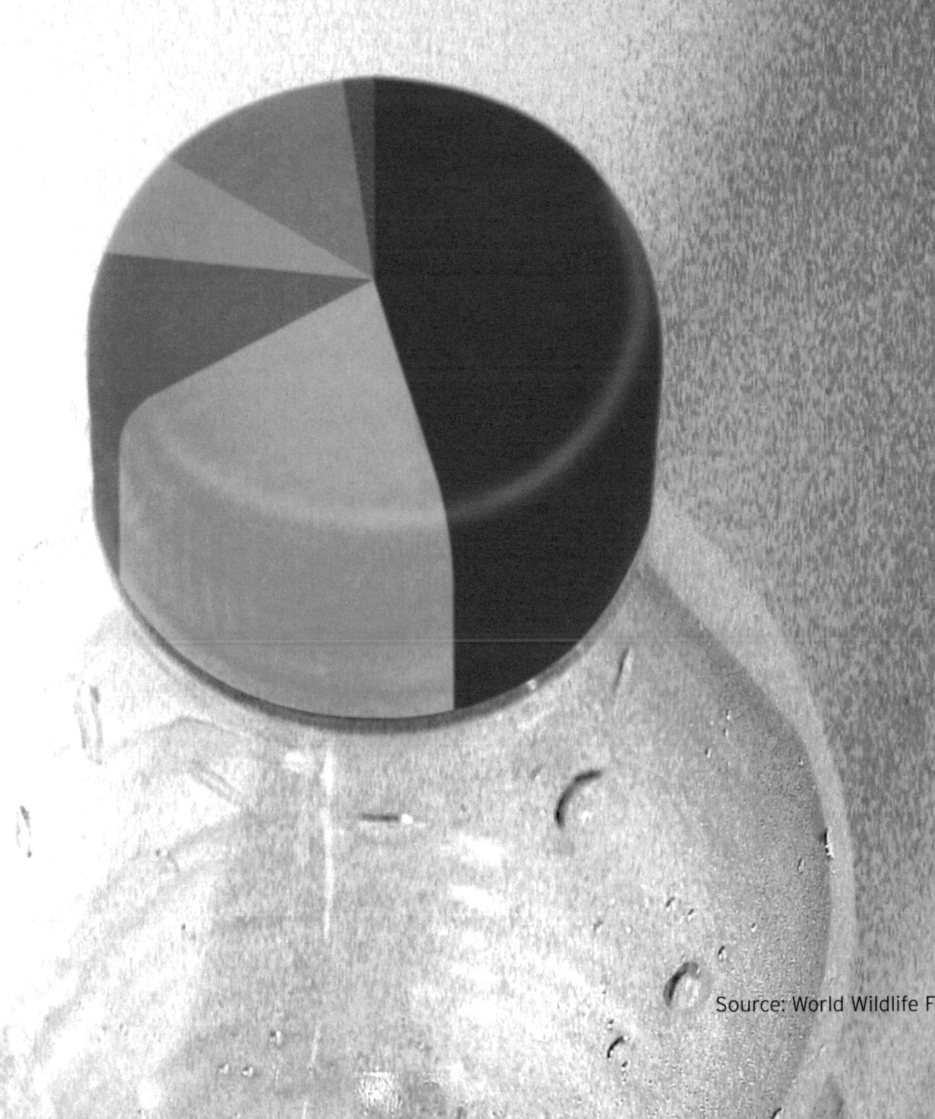

Source: World Wildlife Fund

It takes 50 glasses of water to produce 1 glass of orange juice

12%

OF ALL CASES OF
FOOD POISONING
IN BRITAIN
ARE CAUSED BY
BOTTLED
WATER

AMERICANS EMPTY
2.5 MILLION
PLASTIC WATER BOTTLES AN HOUR.

EACH ONE TAKES 500
YEARS TO DECOMPOSE IF
NOT RECYCLED.

To date, probably the most reliable and widely accepted estimate of the amount of water required to produce a pound of beef is 2,500 gallons per pound.

Newsweek once put it another way...

"THE WATER THAT GOES INTO A 1,000 POUND STEER WOULD FLOAT A DESTROYER."

THE CYCLE OF LIFE IS INTRICATELY TIED UP WITH THE CYCLE OF WATER.

JACQUES COUSTEAU

In 1966, the Hudson River was a national joke, turning color depending on what color they were painting the trucks at the G.M. plant. Now it's a model for ecosystem protection.

08 River of Dreams

Robert F. Kennedy Jr.

The tradition of environmental advocacy I come from says we're not protecting the fish and birds so much for their own sake, but because nature enriches us. Environmental advocacy is about recognizing that we have to preserve the basic infrastructure of natural systems; they connect us to the lands that remind us of our history.

The group that I work for was founded by people who probably never used the label "environmentalists." They were fighting for their community. Riverkeeper was started by a blue-collar coalition of commercial and recreational fishermen who mobilized on the Hudson River in 1966 to reclaim the river from polluters.

> **"We're all downstream."**
> Marq De Villiers

One of the enclaves of commercial fishery on the Hudson is a little village called Crotonville, 30 miles north of New York City on the east bank of the river. The people there in 1966 were not your prototypical tweed-jacketed, affluent environmentalists trying to preserve distant wilderness areas in the Rockies or Montana. They were factory workers, carpenters, electricians. Half the people in Crotonville made at least some of their living crabbing or fishing the Hudson River. For them, the environment was their backyard and the bathing beaches, swimming and fishing holes of the Hudson River. Richie Garrett, the first president of Riverkeeper (then called the Hudson River Fishermen's Association) used to say about the Hudson, "It's our Riviera. It's our Monte Carlo."

In 1964, Penn Central Railroad began vomiting oil from a four-and-a-half-foot pipe in the Croton Harmen rail yard. Oil came up the river on the tides, blackened beaches and made the shad taste of diesel, so that it couldn't be sold at the Fulton Fish Market in the city. Three hundred people in Crotonville came together one night in the Parker-Bale American Legion Hall. Almost all the original founders, board members and officers of Riverkeeper were former Marines – combat veterans

THE CUYAHOGA RIVER BURNS IN 1952.

from World War II and Korea. These weren't radicals or militants, but people whose patriotism was rooted in the bedrock of our country. That night, they started talking about violence because they saw something that they thought they owned - the abundant fisheries that many families had lived on for generations - and the purity of the Hudson's waters being robbed from them by large corporate entities over which they had no control.

They had been to the government agencies that are supposed to protect Americans from pollution and were given the bum's rush. By this evening in March 1966, virtually everybody in Crotonville had come to the conclusion that the government was in cahoots with the polluters, and the only way that they were going to reclaim the river was if they confronted the polluters directly. People variously suggested that they put a match to the oil slick coming out of the Penn Central pipe and blow it up or float a raft of dynamite into the intake of the Indian Point power plant, which at that time was killing a million fish a day.

We give them each four polluters to sue at the beginning of the semester. If they don't win, they don't pass the course.

Bob Boyle was the outdoor editor of *Sports Illustrated* and a Korean War veteran. Two years before, he had written an article about angling in the Hudson and in his research had come across an ancient navigational statute called the 1888 Rivers and Harbors Act, which said that it was illegal to pollute any waterway in the United States. There was also a bounty provision that said that anybody who turned in the polluter got to keep half the fine. He sent a copy of this law over to the libel lawyers at Time, Inc., asking if it was still good. They told him that it hadn't been enforced in 80 years, but it was still on the books. That evening, when these men were talking about violence, he stood up before them with a copy of the law and said, "We shouldn't be talking about breaking the law. We should be talking about enforcing it." They resolved that they were going to start the Fishermen's Association and that they were going to go out and track down and prosecute every polluter on the Hudson.

Eighteen months later they collected the first bounty in U.S. history under this 19th-century statute. They shut down the Penn Central pipe and got to keep $2,000, which was a huge amount in Crotonville in 1968. For two weeks they celebrated, and they used what was left over to go after Ciba-Geigy, Tuck Tape Standard Brand, and American Cyanamide, the largest corporations in America, and the government agencies that are also the worst polluters on the Hudson. In 1973 they collected the highest penalty in U.S. history against a corporate polluter: $200,000 from Anaconda Wire and Cable for dumping toxics at Hastings, New York. They used that money to construct a boat called The Riverkeeper, which today patrols the river. In 1983 they hired a former commercial fisherman named John Cronin as their first full-time Riverkeeper, and he hired me a year later as their prosecuting attorney.

About a year after that at Pace Law School in White Plains, New York, we started a litigation clinic, where we have 10 third-year law students who, by a special court order, are permitted to practice law under our supervision as if they're attorneys. We give them each four polluters to sue at the beginning of the semester. If they don't win, they don't pass the course. We've brought over 300 successful legal actions against Hudson River polluters, forcing them to spend over $2 billion on remediation of the river. Today the Hudson River is an international model for ecosystem protection. It was a national joke in 1966, an open sewer, turning color sometimes three times a week, depending on what color they were painting the trucks at the G.M. plant in Tarrytown. The miraculous resurrection of the Hudson has inspired the creation of Riverkeepers on waterways across North America. Each one of them has a patrol boat, a full-time paid Riverkeeper and attorneys prepared to litigate.

I remember what it was like before Earth Day: The Cuyahoga River burned for a week and nobody was able to put it out; Lake Erie was declared dead; we couldn't swim in the Potomac, the Hudson or the Charles growing up; and some days you couldn't see down the block for the smog. We had thousands of Americans dying in our cities every year from smog events. Young congressmen on Capitol Hill don't remember these days. They only see the cost of environmental regulations, not the benefits that this nation has gotten through investments in our environmental infrastructure.

The administration is now saying we have to choose between economic prosperity and environmental protection. That is a false choice. In 100 percent of the situations, good environmental policy is identical to good economic policy if we want to measure our economy based upon how it produces jobs over the long term. If we treat the planet as if it were a business in liquidation, converting our natural resources to cash as quickly as possible, to have few years of pollution-based prosperity, we can generate an instantaneous cash flow and the illusion of a prosperous economy. But our children are going to pay for our joy ride with denuded landscapes and poor health and huge cleanup costs. Environmental injury is deficit spending.

Robert F. Kennedy Jr. is the chief prosecuting attorney for Riverkeeper, senior attorney for the Natural Resources Defense Council, president of the Waterkeeper Alliance, and a clinical professor at Pace University School of Law.

Big dams are plain bad. They flood people out of their homes and off their lands; wipe out endangered habitats and species; spread water-borne diseases; deprive flood plains of the water and sediments of life-giving floods.

09 Damming It All to Hell

Patrick McCully

Dams ruin beautiful landscapes and submerge places of great cultural and spiritual importance. Big dams even cause earthquakes (because of the weight of water in reservoirs), release greenhouse gases (because of the rotting of flooded vegetation), destroy marine fisheries (because they disrupt river-borne flows of freshwater and nutrients into oceans) and lead to coastal erosion (because the sediments that eventually fill reservoirs would previously have flowed out through estuaries and then been washed back by waves to protect the shoreline). Occasionally, they collapse and drown people. In the world's worst dam disaster – a mega-catastrophe that struck central China in 1975 when two large dams burst – as many as 230,000 people died.

The world's worst dam has to be the gargantuan Three Gorges project in China. It will cause all of the problems above – on a mind-bending scale. More than half a million people had been moved from their homes along the Yangtze by June 2003 when the first stage of filling the Three Gorges reservoir began. By the start of the final phase of reservoir filling in 2008 a further 700,000 people (according to government statistics) will have been evicted. Chinese critics claim the final number will reach nearly 2 million. For their trouble, these critics have been beaten up, imprisoned, and had their books and articles banned.

In the world's worst dam disaster ... as many as 230,000 people died.

Human-rights abuses regularly accompany big dams, and not just in China. In the 1980s, more than 440 Guatemalans, mainly women and children, were murdered by paramilitaries because of their refusal to accept the resettlement package offered by the World Bank-funded electricity utility building the Chixoy dam.

Today, almost everywhere that a big dam is being proposed or built there is a community or a group of activists organizing against it. In southern Mexico, indigenous communities are fighting to win reparations for dams built 50 years ago.

A MARKER INDICATES THE ESTIMATED DEPTH OF WATER EXPECTED WHEN THE THREE GORGES DAM IN CHINA IS COMPLETE.

DAMS HAVE ALTERED THE SPEED OF THE EARTH'S ROTATION, AND THE SHAPE OF ITS GRAVITATIONAL FIELD

While not every big dam causes huge damage, cumulatively the world's 47,000 large dams have done major harm. The World Commission on Dams, a World Bank-sponsored initiative backed by both dam supporters and critics, estimated that 40 to 80 million people have been displaced by dams. Sixty percent of the length of the world's large river systems are at least moderately or severely fragmented by dams and related withdrawals of water for irrigation.

Corruption and the power of the big dam lobby ... has meant that feasibility studies for new dams have regularly underestimated their costs and exaggerated their benefits.

This massive replumbing of the world's rivers is a major reason for the rapid loss of freshwater species. Around a third of freshwater fish species known to have existed are now classified as extinct, endangered or vulnerable. A significant but unknown share of shellfish, amphibians, plants and birds that depend on freshwater habitats are also extinct or at risk.

But aren't dams, like dentists' drills and taxes, just a necessary evil that we must grudgingly accept for our greater good? Don't we need to store water to keep ourselves and our crops alive through dry seasons and dry years? Don't we need to block floods? Don't we need hydroelectricity? We do need to store water. In large parts of the world rain falls only during one or two wet seasons, and within those seasons almost all the rain might fall in just one or two storms. And global warming is making rainfall even less dependable.

But the best form of water storage is in the ground, not in huge surface reservoirs created by damming rivers. Storage in the form of groundwater does not flood homes or habitats, and does not evaporate as does water in reservoirs.

Groundwater is the primary source of drinking water for roughly a third of the world's people and the great majority of rural dwellers. Land irrigated with groundwater tends to be far more productive than that watered from huge dam-and-canal irrigation projects because a farmer can control when they use water from their own well whereas, with big dam irrigation schemes, the quantity and timing of water supplied is at the mercy of an often inefficient and corrupt bureaucracy.

A growing movement, especially in India but also in many other parts of the world, is now seeking to revive and update the age-old practice of augmenting the natural recharge of groundwater by trapping rainfall behind small embankments and dams long enough for it to soak through into the ground. In Rajasthan state alone, around 700,000 people benefit from the improved access to groundwater for household use, farm animals, and crops. Not a single family has been displaced in order to achieve this. Rainwater harvesting also works in urban areas, where rain can be caught on rooftops and channelled into tanks.

While there is no alternative to life-giving water, there are many alternatives to hydroelectricity. To begin with, we can use electricity more efficiently, but also develop new, renewable sources of energy to reduce our dependence on hydroelectricity.

There has never been a fair playing field when dams have been compared with their alternatives. Corruption and the power of the big dam lobby, both in government and corporations, has meant that feasibility studies for new dams have regularly underestimated their costs and exaggerated their benefits. If assessments of options for water and energy needs were made comprehensive, transparent and participatory, very few large dams would make the grade. This is no doubt a major factor in the dam industry's squeals of protest over the recommendations of the World Commission on Dams, which include just such assessments.

History shows that trying to dam our way out of our water problems will just make them worse. It also shows that a better water world is possible.

Patrick McCully is Campaigns Director of International Rivers Network and author of *Silenced Rivers: The Ecology and Politics of Large Dams* (Zed Books 1996 and 2001).

The World Commission on Dams estimated that big dams contribute less than 10 percent to India's grain production.

"Ten percent of the total produce currently works out to 20 million tons. This year [2001], more than double that amount is rotting in government storehouses while at the same time 350 million Indian citizens live below the poverty line. The Ministry of Food and Civil Supplies says that 10 percent of India's total food grain produced every year is spoiled or eaten by rats. India must be the only country in the world that builds dams, uproots millions of people, and submerges thousands of acres of forests in order to feed rats."

Arundhati Roy, *Power Politics*
(South End Press 2001)

Anishinaabekwe, the Daughter,
You are the keepers of the water.
I am Nibi ... water ...the sacred source
The blood of Aki, Mother Earth,
The force filling dry seeds to great bursting.
I am the wombs cradle.
I purify.

Nibi, the life giver.
Forever the Circle's charge
I have coursed through our Mother's Veins.
Now hear my sorrow and my pain
In the river's rush, the rain...

I am your grandchildren's drink
Listen, Daughters, always.
You are the keepers of the water.
Hear my cry,
For the springs flow darkly now
Through the heart of Aki.

American Indian poem,
Ojibwa, Minnesota

38 MILLION INDIGENOUS PEOPLE HAVE BEEN DISPLACED BY 840,000 DAMS WORLDWIDE

60% OF THE WORLD'S RIVERS HAVE BEEN DAMMED

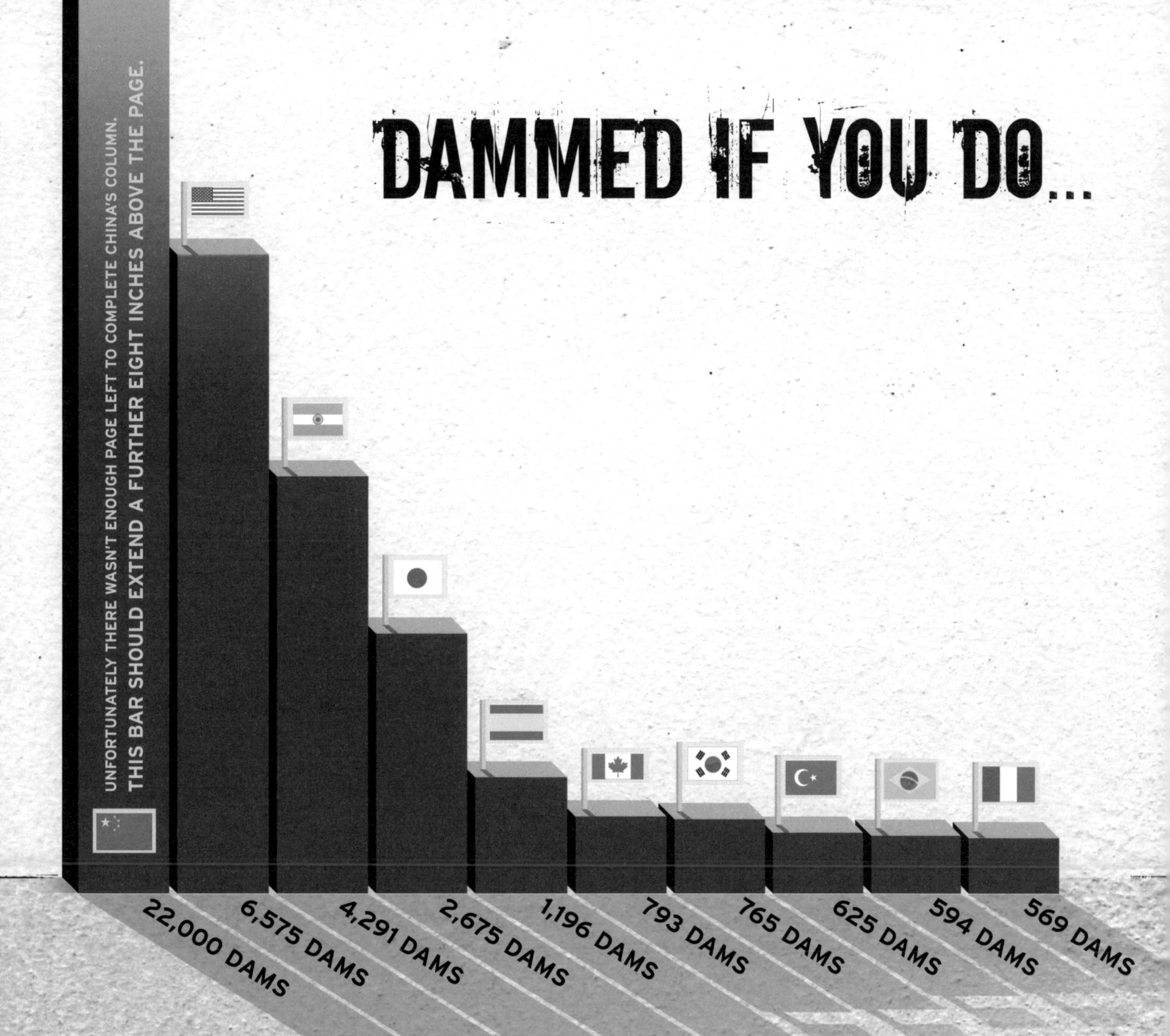

↑ NUMBER OF DAMS → COUNTRIES

WORLD COMMISSION ON DAMS

In Africa, 90 percent of the work of gathering water and wood for the household and for food preparation, is done by women. - UNESCO

10 The Weight of Water

WaterAid

Imagine if every morning you had to get up at the crack of dawn and walk for miles down uneven paths to the nearest water hole to collect your family's water for the day. Then imagine the state of the water: filthy, buzzing with flies; the same source used by wild animals. In many countries it would take you more than six hours every day to collect enough water for your family for a single day's needs. Only upon returning from this grueling journey could you start the rest of your day - farming (women's work in much of the developing world), cooking, keeping house, raising children.

In most developing countries, the task of collecting water falls to women. In rural Africa women often walk 10 miles or more every day to fetch water in containers that can weigh upwards of 50 pounds when full. In the dry season it is not uncommon for women to walk twice this distance. Carrying such weight daily - commonly on the head, back, or hip - is tough on a body. Backache and joint pains are common, and in extreme cases, curved spines and pelvic deformities can result, creating complications in childbirth.

The paths to these wells are often narrow, slippery, and dangerous. The wells at the end of these journeys are often little more than waterholes dug out deeper and deeper as the dry season progresses. They can be very difficult to reach, with steep sides. Sometimes the dirt walls collapse, killing those inside.

In many countries it would take you more than six hours every day to collect enough water for your family for a single day's needs.

Even after traveling such long distances, women often have to wait in queues at the source. Waiting can add five hours onto the journey. Some traditional sources almost dry out for several months each year and it can take up to an hour for one woman to fill her bucket as she waits for the water to slowly filter through the ground. To avoid such long waits, many women get up in the middle of the night to get to the source when demand is low.

WOMEN WAIT IN THE PRE-DAWN LIGHT AT A WATER PUMP IN ZIMBABWE.

After all this, the water they finally gather is often polluted, rife with bacteria and parasites that cause life-threatening diseases such as cholera, dysentery, and guinea worm. Thousands of children under the age of five die, mostly in Africa, every day from waterborne disease.

WaterAid and other charities are working on implementing new water delivery and sanitation systems in developing nations, focusing specifically on involving women in the process.

WaterAid, a UK-based charity, works with communities in developing nations to provide safe, clean, reliable water-delivery and sanitation systems.

This is Lucy's story

She lives in Kandiga, Ghana

A decade ago, I had to get up at 3 a.m. every day to collect water from a river over three miles away. The earliest I returned was 10 a.m., which meant I was often late for work (I am a teacher). Even so, I always went alone so that my children could go to school. Sometimes they had water to wash with and prepare breakfast. Sadly, sometimes they did not. They often went to school late or without food because of my absence.

In my community, women were expected to provide water every morning for their husbands. The lack of water often resulted in quarrels, wife-beating or even divorce. My husband divorced me after quarrels over water.

Fetching water took up most of the women's day. During our dark dawn journey to the river, some women were bitten by snakes, others fell down from fatigue, injuring themselves and breaking their water pots and calabashes. Young girls were also expected to carry water, and so very few enrolled in schools.

In Kandiga, communities suffered most from water shortages during the long dry season from November to March. Because water was so scarce, we were forced to collect dirty water, which posed severe health hazards. Sanitary facilities were generally non-existent. My children and others in the neighborhood were often ill and severely malnourished.

In 1994, I heard about WaterAid. I quickly organized our community and applied for assistance. In 1995, after several meetings, the project was agreed and the first two hand-dug wells were constructed.

On the first day after the handpump was installed I woke up at 6 a.m. and cried aloud, thinking I was too late to fetch water from the river. Then I realized that, in their excitement, my children had woken up earlier and filled the water pots with clean water and were already preparing breakfast.

Since then, life in my community has been peaceful. Fighting, quarrels, snakebites, exhaustion, and water-borne diseases are things of the past.

Men and children fetch water for all their own needs, and there is a remarkable increase in school enrollment for both boys and girls.

Women's lives in particular have been greatly enhanced. We have time to look after our families and earn money by weaving or farming. Previously, we were seen as unintelligent. Now we are seen as equals. We are involved in decision-making and can take up leadership roles – something that was unthinkable before. I have been elected to represent my community in the District Assembly, the highest political authority at the district level. Debates and decision-making have been strengthened, and communities are encouraged to manage local and environmental resources. This, in turn, has led to industry, improved living conditions, and better health.

Life without water used to be awful. I had no time for myself and was always depressed, worrying where I could get water from. I didn't think I was capable of anything. Now I am so surprised by what I can do, I am surprised that I can do it, and I am very happy.

THANKS TO WaterAid FOR ALLOWING USE OF LUCY'S PHOTOGRAPH.

We can't help being thirsty, moving toward the voice of water. Milk drinkers draw close to the mother. Muslims, Christians, Jews, Buddhists, Hindus, shamans, everyone hears the intelligent sound and moves with thirst to meet it.

Rumi

THOUSANDS HAVE LIVED WITHOUT LOVE, NOT ONE WITHOUT WATER.

You don't wash blood away with blood but with water.
Turkish proverb

11 Bombs Away: Water and Warfare

UNESCO

Because it is indispensable to life, water is often at stake during armed conflicts. Since ancient times, the destruction of water resources and facilities has been used as a weapon against the enemy. History is full of such examples from all over the world, showing a great variety of strategies for targeting water in a military conflict:

- In 596 B.C., Nebuchadnezzar breached the aqueduct that supplied the city of Tyre in order to end a long siege.
- In 1503, Leonardo da Vinci and Machiavelli planned to divert the Arno River away from Pisa during a conflict between Pisa and Florence.
- In 1863, during the U.S. Civil War, General Ulysses S. Grant cut levees in Vicksburg to cut off the Confederate army.
- In 1938, Chiang Kai-shek ordered the destruction of flood-control dikes on a section of the Yellow River in order to flood areas threatened by the Japanese army. The flood did kill part of the invading army, but also between 10,000 and 1 million Chinese civilians.
- During World War II (1940 - 1945), hydroelectric dams were routinely bombed as strategic targets.
- During the Vietnam War, many dikes were destroyed or damaged by systematic bombing. North Vietnam claimed a death toll of 2 to 3 million inhabitants due to the drowning or starvation that resulted from these attacks.
- In 1981, Iran bombed a hydroelectric facility serving Iraq, blacking out much of the country.
- In 1993, Saddam Hussein poisoned and drained the water supplies of Shiite Muslims in the South.
- In 1999 in Kosovo, water supplies and wells were intentionally contaminated by Serbs. The same year, a bomb blast destroyed the main pipeline in Lusaka, Zambia, cutting off water to the city and its 3 million inhabitants.

From the UNESCO World Water Assessment Programme

THE HAGUE CONVENTION

Protocol I (art. 54) prohibits, "whatever the motive," the attacking, destroying, removing of "objects indispensable to the survival" of civilian population, such as "drinking water installations and supplies and irrigation works."

Protocol I (art. 56) prohibits attacks against "works and installations containing dangerous forces, namely dams, dikes, and nuclear electrical generating stations."

(The United States was one of a handful of countries which refused to ratify these protocols when they were adopted in 1977.)

Drying Out the Desert

Documents unearthed by professor Thomas J. Nagy of George Washington University show how the United States knowingly used bombings during the first Gulf War and sanctions against Iraq in the decade following to degrade the water infrastructure in that country, despite acknowledging that the result would be widespread death and disease, especially among children.

The U.S. Defense Intelligent Agency (DIA) issued a classified document just before the Gulf War laying out a strategy:

"Iraq depends on importing specialized equipment and some chemicals to purify its water supply. With no domestic sources of both water treatment replacement parts and some essential chemicals, Iraq will continue attempts to circumvent U.N. Sanctions to import these vital commodities. Failing to secure supplies will result in a shortage of pure drinking water for much of the population. This could lead to increased incidences, if not epidemics, of disease."

"... Iraq will suffer increasing shortages of purified water because of the lack of required chemicals and desalination membranes. Incidences of disease, including possible epidemics, will become probable unless the population were careful to boil water. ... Iraq's overall water treatment capability will suffer a slow decline, rather than a precipitous halt. Although Iraq is already experiencing a loss of water treatment capability, it probably will take at least six months before the system is fully degraded."

Just after Desert Storm was launched, another DIA document predicted the health effects on the civilian population:

"Conditions are favorable for communicable disease outbreaks, particularly in major urban areas affected by coalition bombing. ... Infectious disease prevalence in major Iraqi urban areas targeted by coalition bombing (Baghdad, Basrah) undoubtedly has increased since the beginning of Desert Storm. ... Current public health problems are attributable to the reduction of normal preventive medicine, waste disposal, water purification and distribution, electricity, and the decreased ability to control disease outbreaks."

The army is the poison and the people are the water in which the poison is mixed.

Vietnamese proverb

"... the most likely diseases during next 60-90 days (descending order): diarrheal diseases

> (particularly children); acute respiratory illnesses (colds and influenza); typhoid; hepatitis A (particularly children); measles, diphtheria, and pertussis (particularly children); meningitis, including meningococcal (particularly children); cholera (possible, but less likely)."

The documents noted that the Iraqi government would blame the disease outbreaks on the United States, but that the US government should claim that the Iraqis were "propagandizing." They did precisely that.

Nagy also uncovered the Air Force's Doctrine Document 2-1.2, dated May 1998, entitled "Strategic Attack," which includes an analysis of Desert Storm:

> "The loss of electricity shut down the capital's water treatment plants and led to a public health crisis from raw sewage dumped in the Tigris River."

This observation appeared in the section of the report entitled "Elements of Effective Operation."

Professor Thomas J. Nagy wrote the article "The Secret Behind the Sanctions: How the U.S. Intentionally Destroyed Iraq's Water Supply" for *The Progressive* in 2001.

BAGHDAD, IRAQ MARCH 2003.

By means of water, we give life to everything.

Koran, 21:30

Masaru Emoto, a Japanese scientist, believes that water has emotion, soul and memory. His experiments involved playing music for and showing words like "hope," "love," "hate," and "war" to water samples and then photographing the microscopic crystals. His beautiful book *Message From Water* displays his photographs and claims that pollution, rock music, and angry words upset water and alter its molecular form.

Throughout the history of literature, the guy who poisons the well has been the worst of all villains.

Anonymous

“We, the Indigenous Peoples from all parts of the world, reaffirm our relationship to Mother Earth and responsibility to future generations to raise our voices in solidarity to speak for the protection of water. We were placed in a sacred manner on this earth, each in our own sacred and traditional lands and territories to care for all of creation and to care for water.

We recognize, honor and respect water as sacred and sustains all life. Our traditional knowledge, laws and ways of life teach us to be responsible in caring for this sacred gift that connects all life.

Our relationship with our lands, territories and water is the fundamental physical cultural and spiritual basis for our existence. This relationship to our Mother Earth requires us to conserve our freshwaters and oceans for the survival of present and future generations.”

The Indigenous People's
Kyoto Water Declaration, 2003

The conflict between Israel and the Palestinians is, of course, about religion and power and history. But what few outside the region realize is that it is also largely about water.

12 Thirsting for Justice in Palestine

Barbara Stocking, Oxfam Great Britain

In the arid landscape, only water makes life and settlement possible. Oxfam understands the deep fear Israelis have of losing their country and of the horrific suicide bombings they regularly suffer. But we also must hold them accountable for violations of the Geneva Convention which dictates that occupying powers must provide the residents of an occupied territory basic human needs – including water.

The Palestinian village of Madama, a few kilometers from the West Bank town of Nablus, is one of hundreds of Palestinian villages that – unlike most Israeli settlements – are not connected to any water network. Oxfam is assisting some 30 such villages by building cisterns and providing roof and storage tanks.

Madama's 1,700 residents are entirely dependent upon springs for free water. In hot summer months the springs are virtually dry and the villagers must buy water from tankers pulled by tractors.

The springs lie more than a kilometer from Madama up a steep hill, at the top of which the rooftops of the Israeli Yizhar settlement can be seen.

The settlers there have running water in their taps 365 days a year supplied by the Israeli network, Mekorot, a private company that has a virtual monopoly on water distribution in Israel and 43 percent of the West Bank.

The settlers pay about three shekels ($0.65) per cubic meter of water and can use as much as they choose. Madama's inhabitants pay 15 shekels ($3.30) per cubic meter for tankered water, five times as much as their neighbors.

The Israeli human rights group B'Tselem estimates that the average Palestinian West Bank citizen consumes 60 liters of water a day for all household and drinking needs. But Israelis in Israel and in West Bank settlements like Yizhar consume 350 liters per day, according to B'Tselem.

Before the second intifada, 80 percent of Madama's men worked in Israel and were paid up to 120 shekels ($26) a day for laboring jobs. But since the violence began, Israel has clamped down on the number of work entry permits it will issue to Palestinians, and

AN ISRAELI TANK DESTROYS A WATER WELL AND HOME
IN THE GAZA STRIP AFTER A SUICIDE BOMB ATTACK.

unemployment in Madama has gone from virtually nothing to 65 percent.

"When you wash yourself, you have to ask yourself if you can really afford it," said Ayed Kamal, the head of the village council of Madama. "Everyone in this village has to make tough choices. There is much less money in the village now so people have to cut down on everything, and that means water too."

To make matters very much harder, for the fifth time in less than a year, the springs have been vandalized.

"We encased them in concrete and fitted pipes to take the water down to Madama," said Kamal. "When we went there one morning we found the cement, which was still wet, had been hacked away, and what was worse, disposable nappies [diapers], rotting meat and putrid fruit had been tipped into the springs. On top of that, dry cement had been poured in to block the spring altogether."

"Then the settlers shot and wounded three Palestinians trying to repair the damage. They even shot at Oxfam staff trying to mend the pipes."

Kamal got the springs cleaned and reset in thick, deep concrete in October 2003, and he hopes this will be a final repair. Concrete was mixed at a base camp at the bottom of the hill and relayed to Palestinian workers at the springs in buckets carried by donkeys. The work was completed under the protection of unarmed volunteers who acted as human shields, lookouts and guards while the repairs were made.

"This time the volunteers are going to stay until the cement is dry this evening," said Kamal.

Later that evening, he walked down the hill to a tap outside the mosque where villagers collect drinking water. For the first time in months, it gushed clean water.

"This is wonderful," said Kamal. "There'll be celebrations in the village tonight. We have water again, and we are going to throw a party."

Barbara Stocking is the director of Oxfam, Great Britain.

A PALESTINIAN MAN COLLECTS WATER PROVIDED BY THE UNITED NATIONS

A PALESTINIAN BOY CARRIES WATER NEAR A DEMOLISHED HOUSE AT A REFUGEE CAMP

FACT: During the current intifada, the Israeli army has damaged the water infrastructure in 202 Palestinian communities and the water network in 255 Palestinian communities.

Center for Economic and Social Rights

Israeli Security vs. Human Rights

"Often [Israeli measures] appear so disproportionate, so remote from the interest of security, that one is led to ask whether they are not in part designed to punish, humiliate and subjugate the Palestinian people. Israel's legitimate security needs must be balanced against the legitimate humanitarian needs of the Palestinian people. To the Special Rapporteur it appears that there is no such balance. Human rights have been sacrificed to security."

United Nations Special Rapporteur to the Occupied Palestinian Territories, 2002

Palestinian Women and the Right to Water

Water shortage has a particular impact on women. In most homes, women are the water managers and are thus responsible for obtaining water, cleaning it when necessary and making decisions about water use. Women are therefore bearing the increased cost of tankered water, which requires them to engage in income-generating activities for the first time or to sell off jewelry and possessions.

Many women are forced to borrow money and are incurring increasing debts. Women also must bear the increased time needed to provide water for the household as they travel longer distances to access water from springs and spend more time filtering and boiling the spring water which is of a lower quality. Finally, women are making the decisions on how to use increasingly limited water supplies. In some areas this has resulted in bathing children less. Often women's small-scale production activities suffer – they may have to sell land and livestock to purchase water, or have to sell off livestock when they can no longer afford to give them water to drink.

Oxfam Great Britain

Water is a moving,
wandering thing,
and must of
necessity continue
to be common by
the law of nature.
William Blackstone

A RECENT PENTAGON REPORT ON **GLOBAL WARMING** WARNS THAT SEVERAL MAJOR EUROPEAN AND AMERICAN CITIES WILL BE **UNDERWATER** BY THE YEAR **2020**

Rising sea levels, melting ice caps, floods, storms, droughts ... Climate change, caused by the burning of fossil fuels, is already with us, and threatens to change our relationship to water in dramatic, irreversible ways.

13 Rising Tide: The Trouble with Too Much Water

Greenpeace UK

Scientific assessments are stark: The United Nations has predicted that by 2025, increasing drought will mean that 5 billion – 2 out of 3 people in the world – will lack sufficient water, and millions more will starve.

Global warming isn't just about heat waves. Flooding will become more frequent in many parts of the world, and not just in coastal areas; in Europe, river flooding will increase over much of the continent. Already in the United Kingdom and the United States, some insurance companies no longer insure those living in flood-prone areas, including multi-million-dollar oceanfront estates.

Glaciers and polar ice caps are set to continue melting, so that we may lose the Greenland and Antarctic ice sheets completely. New, coldwater influxes from the Arctic into the oceans could trigger a slow down or diversion of the Gulf Stream that gives most of Europe its relatively mild climate. And it is these melting glaciers, along with the thermal expansion of the ocean, that are causing sea levels to creep up year after year.

As sea levels rise, many coastal areas will suffer further flooding and erosion, loss of wetlands and mangroves, and seawater intrusion into freshwater sources. Meanwhile, some coastal ecosystems, including coral reefs, atolls, reef islands, and salt marshes could disappear.

The greatest impacts – of both lack of water and excess of it – will be (and already are) on the world's poorest people in parts of Africa and Asia, those least able to protect themselves from rising sea levels and increased drought and disease.

In the summer of 2003, heat waves were followed by severe flooding in Bangladesh, Sri Lanka, Nepal, Afghanistan, India, China, and Pakistan.

In Bangladesh, researchers fear that the increased rains and floods are the reason that malaria – once eradicated in that country – has returned.

The leaders of Tuvalu – an island country in the Pacific Ocean midway between Hawaii and Australia – have conceded defeat in their battle with the rising

A MAN CARRIES FOOD AND FRESH WATER THROUGH FLOOD WATERS IN MOZAMBIQUE IN 2000.

sea, announcing that the population will abandon their homeland.

As the sea level has risen, Tuvalu has experienced lowland flooding. Saltwater has intruded into its groundwater and contaminated drinking water and cropland. Coastal erosion is eating away at the nine islands that make up the country.

Paani Laupepa, Tuvalu's assistant minister for the environment lays the blame firmly at the door of George W. Bush, who pulled the United States out of the Kyoto Protocol, the only international agreement to reduce carbon emissions: "By refusing to ratify the Protocol, the U.S. has effectively denied future generations of Tuvaluans their fundamental freedom to live where our ancestors have lived for thousands of years," he said.

In 2002, Tuvalu - along with its neighbors Kiribati and the Maldives - announced plans for legal action against the Western nations and corporations which they say are responsible for the global warming that is raising the Pacific's level. Tuvalu's Prime Minister explained: "Flooding is already coming right into the middle of the islands, destroying food crops and trees which were there when I was born 60 years ago. These things are gone. Somebody has taken them. And global warming is the culprit."

Tuvalu is the first country that people have been forced to evacuate because of rising seas, but it almost certainly will not be the last. After Australia balked and refused to accept any Tuvaluan refugees, New Zealand agreed to take in the entire population of 11,000. Australia, like the U.S., has refused to sign on to Kyoto. But a further 311,000 people may be forced to leave the Maldives, and millions of others living in low-lying countries may soon join the flow of climate refugees. Where will they go?

The outlook is certainly bleak, as increasing levels of CO_2 in the atmosphere start to throw our climate and weather patterns off balance, with often catastrophic effects. Yet there are solutions to climate change, and it is water we must turn to for many of the clean alternatives to fossil fuels.

When we think of renewable energy, we tend to think of solar panels and wind turbines. Energy from water however doesn't have to mean large, destructive dams. Wave and tidal power have significant potential to meet our energy needs, and the cutting edge of renewable energy research is currently focusing on these technologies. The remote Scottish island of Islay is home to the world's first commercial wave-power station, generating clean electricity from the mighty waves crashing against its rocky coast. Meanwhile, the UK has just joined pioneers Denmark and Sweden by building its first major wind farm at sea.

Climate change is already showing us that we cannot master nature. But we can harness the power of nature, and the energy within our waves and tides, to stop this problem we have created getting any worse. We must set ourselves on a new path, to replace oil, coal, and gas with clean sources of energy.

PUBLIC FISHING
ROAD
CLOSED

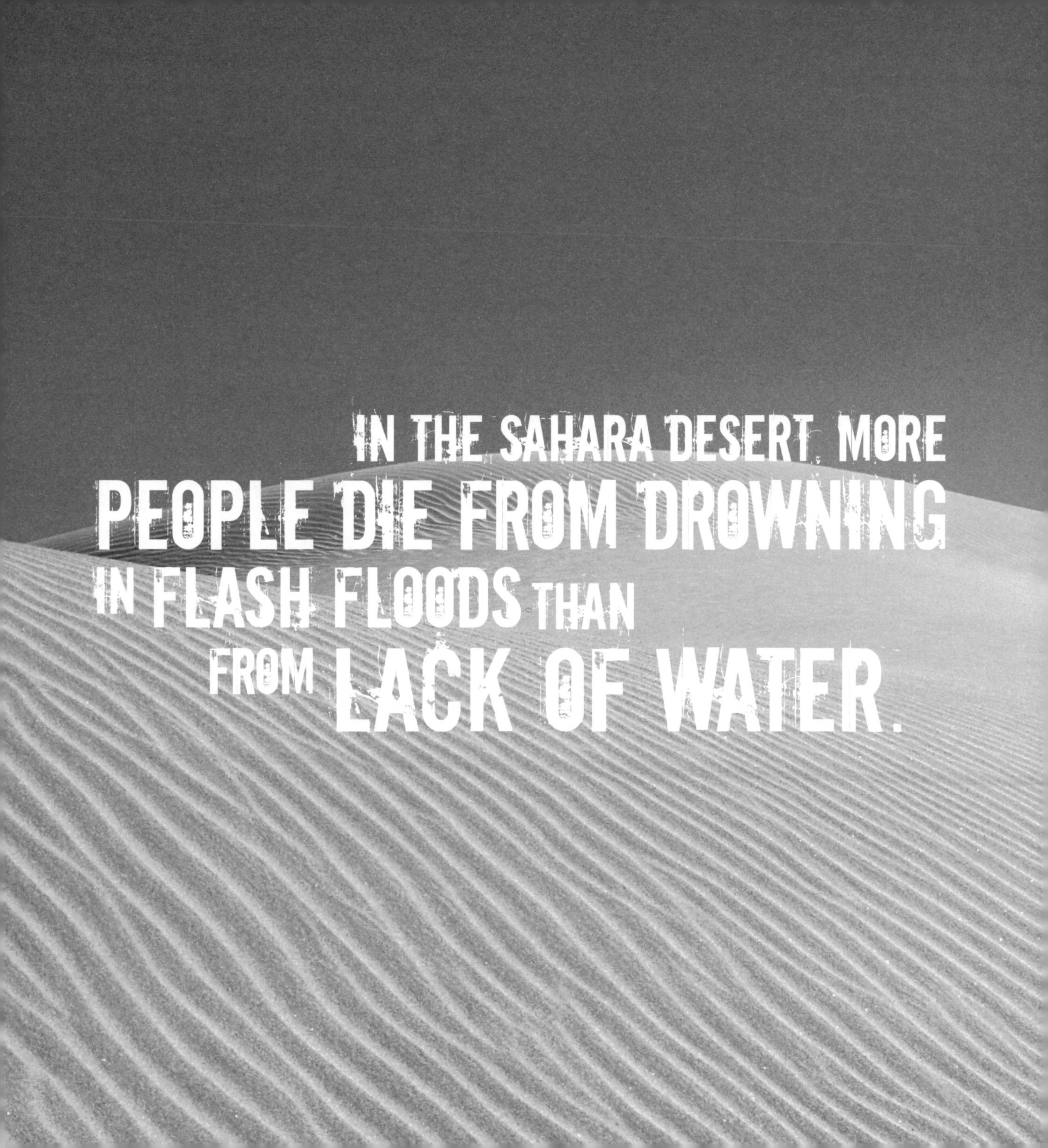

IN THE SAHARA DESERT, MORE PEOPLE DIE FROM DROWNING IN FLASH FLOODS THAN FROM LACK OF WATER.

You could not step twice into the same rivers; for other waters are ever flowing on to you.

Heraclitus of Ephesus

MOZAMBIQUE, 2000.

INUNDATED

Floods throughout Asia in 1998 killed 7,000 people, damaged more than 6 million houses, and destroyed 25 million hectares of cropland in Bangladesh, China, India, and Vietnam.

In September 2000, flooding and landslides in Japan forced the evacuation of 45,000 people; the rainfall was the highest ever recorded in a 24-hour period since records began in 1891.

Also in 2000, heavy rains in Southeast Asia resulted in unprecedented flooding along the Mekong River and its tributaries. Damage was widespread:

- Flood waters inundated parts of northern Thailand, damaging more than half a million hectares of cropland. Nearly half a million people in the Mekong Delta (in Cambodia and Vietnam) had to abandon their homes.
- In Cambodia, rising flood waters submerged close to 400,000 hectares of cropland; emergency food supplies were distributed to 1.4 million people.
- In Lao People's Democratic Republic, more than 18,000 families had to be evacuated from flood plains. The rampaging waters severely damaged nearly 50,000 hectares of cropland.

The UN's Economic and Social Commission for Asia and the Pacific (ESCAP) blamed the floods (and droughts) in the region on widespread deforestation in watershed areas, poor soil management practices, reclamation of flood plains and wetlands for other uses, and the rapid expansion of urban areas.

Source: UNESCO

THE AVERAGE AMOUNT

OF WATER

USED BY 60,000 THAI VILLAGERS PER DAY:

6,500 CUBIC METERS

THE AVERAGE AMOUNT

OF WATER

USED BY ONE GOLF COURSE
IN THAILAND PER DAY:

6,500

CUBIC
METERS

To drink a glass of water, a third of humanity turns on the tap. The rest improvises.

14 Watering the Grassroots: Some Solutions

Dame Anita Roddick

People desperate to survive come up with solutions to problems, because they have no choice. Because more than a billion people worldwide lack access to clean drinking water, some resort to stealing it, while others devise genius plans to outwit profiteers, polluters and even nature.

In Lebanon, it's quite common to illegally siphon off rivers and open ditches. This kind of water is fine for toilets, crops and even laundry. But in Peru, 10 percent of people drink it. In India, some people get treated water by draining holding tanks or bypassing water meters. In Filipino slums, people often rig garden hoses to fire hydrants or pierce city mains.

Those not clever or bold enough to steal are stuck with a rather bad deal. Water trucks often supply slum areas of major cities. But not for free. Dealers serving the shantytowns of Bangladesh are known to charge 250 times the price of municipal water. Such conditions encourage black markets. In Mexico, the water trucked to squatter towns is officially free, but drivers routinely extort and pocket payment.

Poor people in rural areas of Southeast Asia and Africa pay an average of 12 times as much for each liter of water as those connected to municipal systems, spending 20 percent of their income on water.

Dealers serving the shantytowns of Bangladesh are known to charge 250 times the price of municipal water.

It's the sort of entrepreneurialism you don't want to hear about.

In a given weekend, more than 50,000 people around the world will die from diseases triggered by lack of safe drinking water.

While we debate and analyze the statistics of woe, poor people are quietly getting on with the business of finding, getting and keeping clean water. People left to their own devices have to come up with creative solutions, and there are lots of them.

TENDING A MIST NET IN CHILE.

Groundwater, the unseen source of life for most of us, is diminishing almost everywhere in the world. Some 2 billion people and as much as 40 percent of agriculture is at least partly reliant on these hidden stores. And it's costly to extract. Most effort and expense has traditionally gone into schemes to draw up the water from underground sources after it has fallen to earth.

In Kenya, however, they're taking a different approach. As 50 percent of the people of Kenya have no access to safe and adequate water, a group of individuals formed the Kenya Rainwater Association to collect rainwater.

How does it work? Roofs provide the least expensive way of harvesting rain. But it's best done with cheap materials that can be fashioned into household tanks – corrugated iron, plastic, or tile. They build to a general model – foundations sealed with concrete; round tank walls, because these are stronger than rectangular ones; a cover to stop evaporation and prevent contamination. Sounds simple to us, but Kenya is a country where manufactured goods are scarce.

And good practice is copied everywhere. Now, rich countries like Australia and Japan are starting to collect rainwater, thanks to the leading edge technology developed by the Kenya Rainwater Association. Today, there are more than 300 women's groups involved in rainwater harvesting in Kenya, and the technology is being transferred to neighboring Uganda.

Thanks to water harvesting, villages in the Indian district of Madhya Pradesh have avoided the impact of the recent drought that has devastated much of Western India. Water harvesting is a sustainable approach to an age-old problem of seasonal drought.

The inhabitants of Chugungo, a small village of Chile, suffered from water shortages for years, and thus had to carry water from distant sources, and to pay for it. But they have come up with an innovative solution. Huge plastic mesh nets trap the fog; the condensed droplets fall into gutters, and then run through pipelines down the mountains to the village, where the inhabitants have constructed water tanks. These mistnets have provided sufficient good-quality water to meet the basic needs of the villagers, and have allowed them to cultivate four hectares of community vegetable garden.

Some developing countries lucky enough not to suffer from drought, instead suffer the curse of too much water or disease-ridden water. Unsafe drinking water is the world's no. 1 killer, according to the United Nations. Nearly 250 million cases of water-related disease and between 5 million and 10 million deaths occur each year.

Bangladesh, a country of 112 million, is at the forefront of the world water crisis. The poorest there are the most vulnerable, not only to storms and floods, but to water-borne diseases, poor sanitation and arsenic-laced water.

Water can be sterilized by boiling, but this is uneconomical because wood for fuel is extremely scarce in Bangladesh. So, women know that they've just got to do it themselves. Villagers collect water using their saris as filtration tools in an attempt to reduce the occurrence of cholera.

The women have learned from experience just how to do it: The sari needs to be folded so that there are four to eight layers of cloth. The folded cloth is then wrapped over the water pot before water is collected from the river or pond. Laboratory tests have shown that this method removes 99 percent of bacteria.

Saris are found in every household in Bangladesh. They're thin and easy to dry. Water collection using saris to filter out bacteria is an effective method that's available to even the poorest of the poor.

I think the solution that grabs me the most is the children's play pump in South Africa. Children at Thabong nursery school in Davieton, east of Johannesburg, have no idea that they are involved in a scheme that benefits their community.

But the fact is that the community has harnessed the energy of children at play to ease the burden on their mothers. Instead of pumping the water by hand, the children are doing it for them, purely by pushing around and riding on the simple roundabout, or merry-go-round, like the ones we all knew as kids. All that's needed to operate the pump is the energy of children at play. And it's an idea that's spreading throughout the poor villages and deprived urban areas of South Africa.

Fifty-two roundabouts have already been built. How do they work? I'm reliably informed that the roundabouts go round and round and the pump goes up and down. It pumps 1,400 liters an hour. It's as simple as that.

Who pays for it? It's about $5,000 to install the pump and roundabout. Most communities are too poor to afford that. To raise money, the community leases out its water tower for billboard advertising. Major advertisers pay the roundabout company a monthly ad rental, enabling the roundabout company to effectively put the equipment in for free. It's a win-win situation. They're even using the towers to put up messages about the danger of HIV/AIDS prevention. In Africa especially, locales that have problems with water often have problems with HIV.

The technology is transferable all over the world. To me, it's a case of necessarily reinventing the wheel.

It's my belief that worldwide initiatives focus too much on large-scale funding and not enough on small-scale efficiency gains that could reap rewards through community initiatives such as rainwater harvesting. And most World Bank funding still goes towards providing water and sanitation in urban areas where richer people live. It would be cheaper and more effective to approach these solutions on the community level, borrowing from the local wisdom and custom.

For example, it cost $90 million to hold the recent Earth Summit in Johannesburg in 2002, so

CHILDREN AT PLAY IN SOUTH AFRICA PROVIDE
AN ENTIRE VILLAGE WITH FRESH WATER.

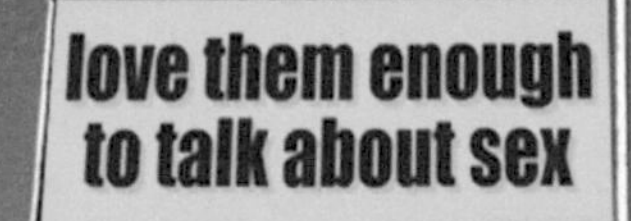

PHOTO COURTESY OF ROUNDABOUT OUTDOOR (www.roundabout.co.za).

"experts" could sit around and talk about theories. In Ethiopia, that would buy 121,000 public water points, at $750 each, each providing enough water for 500 people. That's enough water for Ethiopia's entire 67 million population.

When it comes to private utilities, the reputations of big water companies have been badly damaged by high-profile failures. And in a way, the poor are to blame. The fundamental problem is that the poor are not profitable. They cannot afford to pay for the connection or to pay for consuming enough water to cover operating costs.

In the face of all this failure and inertia, many of the real innovations are taking place at the community level, often spontaneously, or through dynamic cooperation between voluntary groups, small-scale entrepreneurs, and officialdom.

In a small southern Indian project, small vacuum pumps are attached to bicycles. Operated by two or three people, they are used to clear out septic tanks, using affordable and locally appropriate technology. This develops local capacity to solve problems and stops wealth leeching out of the area when foreign consultants and water and civil engineering companies come knocking.

Organizations like the Intermediate Technology Development Group in Britain advocate small-scale solutions to the problems of poverty. Its approach achieves what is impossible for the big water companies, which must answer first to their distant global shareholders. It tries to understand water from the view of poor people who make no distinction between the water they need for drinking and cooking and the supplies they put to productive uses, such as watering livestock, gardens or crops.

Some of my favorite creative solutions to coping with water shortages come from around the world:

- One family in the U.S. bought a king-size waterbed and filled it with distilled water. During water shortages they will have 1,500 liters of drinking water on reserve.

- In Warsaw, Poland, many people wait until water is cheaper (from 10:20 p.m. to 6:20 a.m.) to shower and clean.

- In Kunming, China, residents cover outdoor taps with metal boxes and lock them to prevent theft.

- Hungarian farmers prefer raising chickens and pigs instead of cows, because they require less water.

IN STIGOMTA SWEDEN THEY HOLD AN ANNUAL
"PEE OUTSIDE DAY" WHERE NOBODY
FLUSHES A TOILET
THEY SAVE A FULL 50%
OF THE WATER THE TOWN WOULD TYPICALLY USE IN A DAY

We declare these truths to be universal and indivisible:

15 Water for All

A Declaration from Public Citizen

Water is a common good, the trust of all humanity. The right to water is an inalienable individual and collective right. Each member of the human community has the right to water in quantity and quality sufficient to life and basic economic activities. Water belongs to the Earth and all species and therefore, must not be treated as a private commodity to be bought, sold, and traded for profit.

The intrinsic value of the Earth's water precedes its utility and commercial value and therefore must be respected and safeguarded by all political, commercial and social institutions. Creating the conditions necessary to ensure access to water for the vital needs of every person and every community is an obligation of society as a whole, and the collective responsibility of citizens of the world.

The global water supply is a shared legacy, a public trust and a fundamental human right, and, therefore, a collective responsibility. Only through a high degree of democracy at local, national and international levels, which recognizes these principles, can an equitable and sustainable water policy be created.

And,

Whereas, the world's finite supply of available water is being polluted, diverted, extracted and depleted so fast that millions of people and species are now deprived of water for life,

And,

Whereas governments around the world have failed to protect their precious water legacies,

Therefore,

Citizen organizations in the U.S. join with people around the world to declare the Earth's water supply to be a global commons, to be protected nurtured and judiciously managed by all peoples, communities and all levels of government. Furthermore, we declare that water should never be privatized, commodified, traded, or exported for commercial purpose. It must immediately be exempted from all existing and future international and bilateral trade, investment, credit, and other agreements, including all credit agreements between governments and the International Monetary Fund (IMF), World Bank and other multilateral banks. Because the world's water supply is a common asset, it should not be sold by any institution, government, individual, or corporation for profit.

We advocate immediate action by the U.S. government to be a party to an international treaty, signed by nation states and Indigenous Peoples, to administer the Earth's fresh water supply as a trust. Additionally, because citizens must be at the center of any decision making process, citizen organizations will establish a World Water Parliament.

Along with our partners globally, we call upon governments all over the world to take immediate action to declare that the waters in their territories are a public good and enact strong regulatory structures to protect them from over-use and abuse. Because the world's water supply is a global commons, it must not be sold as a commodity by any institution, government, individual or corporation for profit. The IMF, World Bank and other multilateral banks should not impose water privatization on governments as a condition to access credit.

U.S. Signatures

- Alliance for Democracy
- Americans for Democratic Action, Southern California Chapter
- Center for Economic and Social Rights
- Concerned Citizens Committee of SE Ohio
- Essential Action
- Global Exchange
- Global Resource Action Center for the Environment (GRACE)
- Globalization Challenge Initiative
- Keepers of the Duck Creek Watershed
- Public Citizen
- Resource Center of the Americas
- Waterkeeper Alliance

International Signatures

- Community Information Association, Brisbane, Australia
- Council of Canadians' Blue Planet Project
- International Forum on Globalization
- Institute for Agriculture and Trade Policy
- WTO Watch Qld, Brisbane, Australia

To sign-on to the declaration, please contact: cmep@citizen.org

Public Citizen is a national, nonprofit consumer advocacy organization founded by Ralph Nader in 1971 to represent consumer interests in Congress, the executive branch and the courts.

THE AVERAGE AMERICAN HOME USES **293** GALLONS OF WATER A DAY

THE AVERAGE AFRICAN FAMILY USES

GALLONS OF WATER A DAY

CHILDREN WASH AND COLLECT WATER FROM A STANDPIPE IN BURUNDI.

Resources

Polaris Institute
Polaris is designed to enable citizen movements to re-skill and retool themselves to fight for democratic social change in an age of corporate-driven globalization. Essentially, the Institute works with citizen movements in developing the kinds of strategies and tactics required to unmask and challenge the corporate power that is the driving force behind governments concerning public policy making on economic, social and environmental issues. Director Tony Clarke, co-author of Chapter 2 ("The Lords of Water") and Chapter 7 ("Evian Backward is naïve"), has joined with Maude Barlow to publish several books on the global water crisis.

312 Cooper Street
Ottawa, Ontario
K2P 0G7, Canada
Tel: 613 237 1717
Fax: 613 237 3359
Email: polarisinstitute@on.aibn.com
Web: www.polarisinstitute.org
Operation Water Rights Project:
www.polarisinstitute.org/polaris_project/water_lords/water_lords_index.html

Rainwater Harvesting
Useful tips and practical advice.

Web: www.rainwaterharvesting.org

The Democracy Center
The Democracy Center provides advocacy training, counseling, strategy planning and other assistance to hundreds of groups and thousands of people working on social and economic justice issues on three continents. Executive director Jim Shultz, author of Chapter 3 ("The Blue Revolution"), runs the center from Cochabamba, Bolivia, where he spearheaded a popular revolt against water privatization.

PO Box 22157, San Francisco,
CA 94122, USA or
Casilla 5283, Cochabamba, Bolivia
Tel: 415 564 4767
Fax: 978 383 1269
Email: info@democracyctr.org
Web: www.democracyctr.org

LifeWater International
A Christian charity dedicated to providing safe drinking water and sanitation systems to developing countries.

PO Box 3131, San Luis Obispo,
CA 93403, USA
Tel: 805 541 6634
Fax: 805 541 6649
Email: info@lifewater.org

International Rivers Network
IRN supports local communities working to protect their rivers and watersheds. We work to halt destructive river development projects, and to encourage equitable and sustainable methods of meeting needs for water, energy and flood management. Patrick McCully, author of Chapter 9 ("Damming It All to Hell"), is the IRN's campaign director.

1847 Berkeley Way
Berkeley, CA 94703, USA
Tel: 510 848 1155
Fax: 510 848 1008
Email: info@irn.org
Web: www.irn.org

Riverkeeper
Riverkeeper's mission is to protect the environmental, recreational and commercial integrity of the Hudson River and its tributaries, and to safeguard New York City's and Westchester County's drinking water supply. Chief counsel Robert F. Kennedy, Jr. contributed Chapter 8 ("River of Dreams").

PO Box 130, Garrison,
NY 10524, USA
Tel: 800 21-RIVER
Email: info@riverkeeper.org
Web: www.riverkeeper.org

Greenpeace

This international organization dedicated to the direct-action defense of the environment from whales to genetically modified foods to illegal logging is also dedicated to protecting the universal human right to clean water. Our friends at Greenpeace UK contributed Chapter 13 ("Rising Tide: The Trouble with Too Much Water") about climate change to this book.

Greenpeace International
Ottho Heldringstraat 5
1066 AZ Amsterdam
The Netherlands
Tel: +31 20 5148150
Fax: +31 20 5148151
Email:
supporter.services@int.greenpeace.org
Web: www.greenpeace.org
Climate Change Campaign:
www.greenpeace.org/international_en/campaigns/intro?campaign_id=3937

WaterAid

WaterAid is an international NGO dedicated exclusively to the sustainable provision of safe domestic water, sanitation and hygiene education to the world's poorest people. WaterAid contributed Chapter 10 ("The Weight of Water").

Prince Consort House, 27-29 Albert Embankment, London
SE1 7UB, UK
Tel: 020 7793 4500
Fax: 020 7793 4545
Email: wateraid@wateraid.org
Web: www.wateraid.org

The People's Water Forum

A populist Coalition formed to challenge the World Water Forum - an alliance of multinational water monopolists, the World Bank, and the International Monetary Fund.

X-5, Hauz Khas
New Delhi, India
Tel: 91 11 2696 8077
Fax: 91 11 2656 2093
Email: pwwf@pwwf.org
Web: pwwf.org

UNESCO Water

The United Nations Educational Scientific and Cultural Organization's clearinghouse for international water-related resources. UNESCO contributed facts throughout the book, including Chapter 11 ("Bombs Away: Water and Warfare").

Email: waterportal@unesco.org
Web: www.unesco.org/water

Natural Resources Defense Council

The NRDC defends natural places, systems, and creatures through the legal system, legislation and lobbying, and grassroots organizing. One of its primary foci is clean water and oceans.

40 West 20th Street
New York, NY 10011, USA
Tel : 212 727 2700
Fax: 212 727 1773
Email: nrdcinfo@nrdc.org
Web: www.nrdc.org

Council of Canadians

Founded in 1985, The Council of Canadians is Canada's pre-eminent citizens' watchdog organization, focusing on public interest issues related to globalization. Chair Maude Barlow, co-author of Chapter 2 ("The Lords of Water") and Chapter 7 ("Evian Backward is naïve") is a leading thinker on global water issues.

502-151 Slater Street
Ottowa, Ontario
K1P 5H3, Canada
Tel: 613 233 2773 or 800 387 7177
Fax: 613 233 6776
Email: inquiries@canadians.org
Web: www.canadians.org

WaterPartners International

WaterPartners International is an NGO committed to providing clean drinking water to communities in developing countries.

PO Box 22680
Kansas City, MO 64113-0680, USA
Tel: 913 312 8600
Email: info@water.org
Web: www.water.org

World Commission on Dams

A collaboration of activists, engineers and bureaucrats to study and debate the controversial global issues surrounding the construction of large dams. With its final report in 2000 it disbanded, but remains one of the most influential organizations ever to convene on the subject.

Web: dams.org or unep-dams.org

Global Resistance - India Resource Center

India Resource Center works to support movements against corporate globalization in India and is a project of Global Resistance. Global Resistance works to strengthen the movement against corporate globalization by supporting and linking local, grassroots struggles against globalization around the world. Coordinator Amit Srivastava is author of Chapter 6 ("Coca-Colanization").

7404 Potrero Avenue, El Cerrito,
CA 94530, USA
Email: indiaresource@igc.org
Web: www.GlobalResistance.org
or www.IndiaResource.org

Oxfam

Oxfam International is a confederation of 12 organizations working together in more than 100 countries to find lasting solutions to poverty, suffering and injustice. Among its campaigns are efforts to restore clean water and sanitation systems in war-torn areas such as Palestine and Iraq. Barbara Stocking, director of Oxfam UK, contributed Chapter 12 ("Thirsting for Justice in Palestine").

Oxfam House
274 Banbury Road
Oxford
OX2 7DZ, UK
Tel: 0870 333 2700
Web: oxfam.org.uk

Public Citizen

Public Citizen is an American nonprofit consumer advocacy organization founded in 1971 by Ralph Nader to represent consumer interests in Congress, the executive branch and the courts. Its Critical Mass Energy and Environment Program includes campaigns against global water privatization. Public Citizen contributed Chapter 15 ("Water for All").

215 Pennsylvania Avenue,
SE Washington, DC 20003, USA
Tel: 202 546 4996
Email: CMEP@citizen.org
Web: citizen.org/cmep/Water

Stockholm International Water Institute

A policy think tank that contributes to international efforts to combat the world's escalating water crisis.

Hantverkargatan 5
112 21 Stockholm
Sweden
Tel: 46 8 522 139 60
Fax: 46 8 522 139 61
Email: siwi@siwi.org
Web: www.siwi.org

Oz GREEN

Supporting the World's Waterways in the forms of local, national and international projects.

Email: ozgreen@ozgreen.org.au
Web: www.ozgreen.org.au

The Gender and Water Alliance

A network of 300 organizations and individuals from around the world advising NGOs and governments on the role of women in water management in developing countries. It is an Associated Program of the Global Water Partnership funded by the governments of the Netherlands and United Kingdom.

PO Box 2869
2601 CW
Delft, The Netherlands
Tel: 31 15 219 2943
Fax: 31 15 219 0955
Email: ruhi@genderandwateralliance.org
Web: www.genderandwateralliance.org

Water for People

An international, nonprofit development organization working on safe drinking water and sanitation systems in developing countries. It is a project of the American Water Works Association.

6666 W. Quincy Ave.
Denver, CO 80235, USA
Tel: 303 734 3490
Fax: 303 734 3499
Email: info@waterforpeople.org
Web: waterforpeople.org

National Pure Water Association

A UK-based group campaigning for safe drinking water in Britain.

12 Dennington Lane, Crigglestone,
Wakefield, WF4 3ET, UK
Tel: 01924 254433
Web: www.npwa.freeserve.co.uk

AidWatch

An NGO spearheading the Right to Water campaign in Australia.

19 Eve St Erskineville NSW 2043, Australia
Tel: 61 02 9557 8944
Fax: 61 02 9557 9822
Email: aidwatch@aidwatch.org.au
Web: www.aidwatch.org.au

Christian Aid

Christian Aid believes in strengthening people to find their own solutions to the problems they face. It strives for a new world transformed by an end to poverty and campaigns to change the rules that keep people poor. They have been active in helping war-affected areas regain freshwater access and sanitation.

35 Lower Marsh, Waterloo, London SE1 7RL, UK
Tel: 020 7620 4444
Fax: 020 7620 0719
Email: info@christian-aid.org
Web: www.christian-aid.org.uk

People for Promoting Rainwater Utilization

An NGO campaigning to promote the use of rainwater worldwide to combat shortages and pollution issues.

1-8-1 Higashi Mukojima Sumida-ku, Tokyo 131-0032
Tel: 81-3-3611-0573
Fax: 81-3-361-0574
Web: www.rain-water.org

WaterCan

WaterCan helps citizens of developing countries build sustainable water supply and sanitation services, and encourages Canadians to lend support.

321 Chapel Street, Ottawa, Ontario, K1N 7Z2, Canada
Tel: 613 230 5182 or 1 800 370 5658
Fax: 613 230 0712
Email: info@watercan.com
Web: www.watercan.com

Water Matters

Coordinated by TEAR Australia and is endorsed by the Australian Council for Overseas Aid (ACFOA) lobbies for safe water provision worldwide.

PO Box 164 (1/4 Solwood Lane), Blackburn, VIC 3130, Australia
Tel: 03 9877 7444 or 1800 244 986
Fax: 03 9877 7944
Email: watermatters@tear.org.au
Web: www.watermattersaustralia.org

Australian Conservation Foundation

Campaigning to increase the protection of oceans and water resource management.

Floor 1, 60 Leicester Street, Carlton, VIC 3053, Australia
Tel: 61 03 9345 1111
Fax: 61 03 9345 1166
Web: www.acfonline.org.au

The World's Water

A project of the Pacific Institute, a clearinghouse for information on the world's freshwater resources.

Web: www.worldwater.org

Friends of the Earth International

This environmental organization has a special Water and Wetlands defense campaign.

Web: www.foei.org/water

The WorldWatch Institute

An independent research body focused on environmental and social justice. Research areas include oceans, freshwater systems, water shortages, water-related conflicts and more.

1776 Massachusetts Ave., NW Washington, DC 20036-1904, USA
Tel: 202 452 1999
Fax: 202 296 7365
Email: worldwatch@worldwatch.org
Web: worldwatch.org

Picture Credits

Photography

Still pictures:
Truchet/UNEP 36; Ron Giling 40; Jim Holmes 47; J Tanodra/UNEP 63; Minbuza 93; David Woodfall 102; Per-Anders Pettersson/UNEP 113, 118; Silpngamiert-UNEP 123; Gil Moti 124; Glen Christian 133

Panos Pictures:
Crispin Hughes 12-13, 105; Gerd Ludwig/Visum/Panos 32; Trygve Bolstad 89

Reuters:
David Mercado 23; Ahmed Jadallah 106 ; Suhaib Salem 107

Photodisc/Getty Images:
26-27, 33, 39, 60, 84-85, 92, 103, 109, 115, 130-131, 143

Stockbyte:
31, 59, 132

Biosphoto:
Phone © Sanna Mauro 35; BIOS © Gourlan/Kodak Pro 44

Science Photo Library:
David Nunuk 50-51; Digital Globe/Eurimage 97; Alexis Rosenfeld 98-99

Additional photography:
H.Davies/Exile Images 9; Tom Kruse 24-25; Steven Benson Photography 43, 79; Eric L Wheater/Lonely Planet Images 57; James Thomas/Cleveland State University Library 75; Brent Stirton/RPM (with thanks to WaterAid) 91; Roundabout Outdoor (PTY) Ltd 127

Illustration

Wheelhouse Creative:
Lise Meyrick IFC, 4-5; Lise Meyrick/Leonardo "Uomo Vitruviano", Venezia Gallerie dell' Accademia. Reproduced with permission of the Ministry for Cultural Assets and Activities 28-29; Lise Meyrick/Getty Images 60; Lise Meyrick/Getty Images 61; Lise Meyrick 67; Lise Meyrick/Getty Images 83; Lise Meyrick/Getty Images 95; Lise Meyrick/Getty Images 100-101; Lise Meyrick/Getty Images 119; Lise Meyrick/Getty Images 120-121

James Sparkes/Getty images Front cover; James Sparkes 11, 14-15, 17, 19, 30, 52-53, 65, 69, 70-71, 72, James Sparkes/Getty images 80, James Sparkes 86, 87

Keith Wilson 20-21; Keith Wilson/Getty Images 55; Keith Wilson 66-67; Keith Wilson/Getty Images 73, Keith Wilson/Getty Images 84-85; Keith Wilson/Getty Images 110-111; Keith Wilson/Getty Images 116-117; Keith Wilson/Getty Images 129

Emily Philips 49, 68

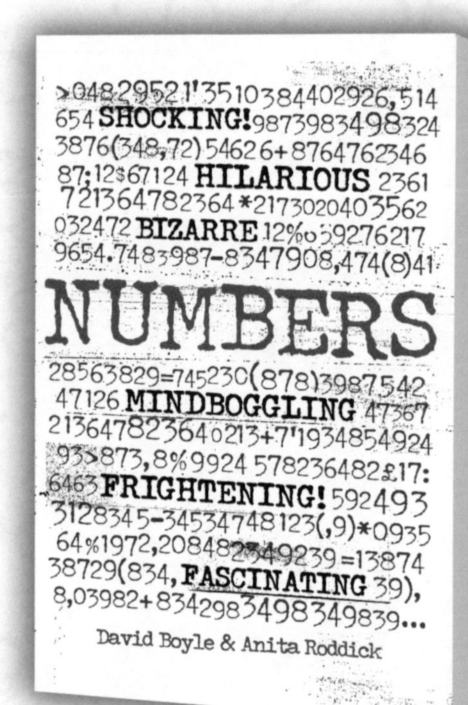

Numbers are peculiar animals. They can unlock secrets, split atoms, reveal the inner workings of people and machines, or draw patterns of jaw-dropping complexity and beauty. In the East, they have mystical significance – they can tell the future and are the key to the secret harmonies of the universe.

NUMBERS

This book encourages a healthy skepticism toward those who would have us quantify the universe and all its minutiae, including our own humanity. You don't have to be a math geek to appreciate this collection of some of the most peculiar, bizarre, shocking, or hilarious numbers we could find. They are meant to make you think, to make you laugh, to move you to action, or simply to entertain.

ISBN: 0-954 3959-2-1
Retail Price: UK £4.99 US $8.95 Paperback

The concept of kindness is often perceived as a passive, squishy, weak quality. We must reclaim this word and the meaning of it from those who would suggest that it is merely a quality we should "practice randomly." Kindness should not be random; kindness should be deliberate and bold and aggressive. Real kindness is active and alive.

A REVOLUTION IN KINDNESS

WHAT WE NEED NOW IS A REVOLUTION IN KINDNESS.

This moving, unexpected, and eclectic collection of essays by celebrities, soldiers, political prisoners, down-and-outs, doctors, philosophers, activists and musicians, is part mosaic and part manifesto. Taken together, these intimate self-portraits make the joyful argument that kindness is not just something to be practiced randomly, but a truly revolutionary idea that really can change the world.

ISBN: 0-9543959-1-3
Retail Price: UK £7.99, US $12.95
(Volume, non-profit, and educational discounts available. Please call for pricing.)
From U.S. telephones: 1-800-423-7087
From U.K. telephones: 0800 018 5450
Or visit www.AnitaRoddick.com

get **informed,**
get **outraged,**
get **inspired,**
get **active!**

AnitaRoddick.com is eclectic, full of personal essays, quirky links, breaking news, and activist information. Updated regularly, Anita's site is an active and well-regarded site in the world of weblogging.

Whether she is filing dispatches from the Amazon rainforest, or soliciting tongue-in-cheek spoofs of corporate logos, or pillorying world leaders for their war-like ways, Anita's website is a peek into the mind of a woman, an entrepreneur, an activist, a grandmother, a curious and concerned global citizen. It is full of joy and passion, outrage and information.

www.AnitaRoddick.com

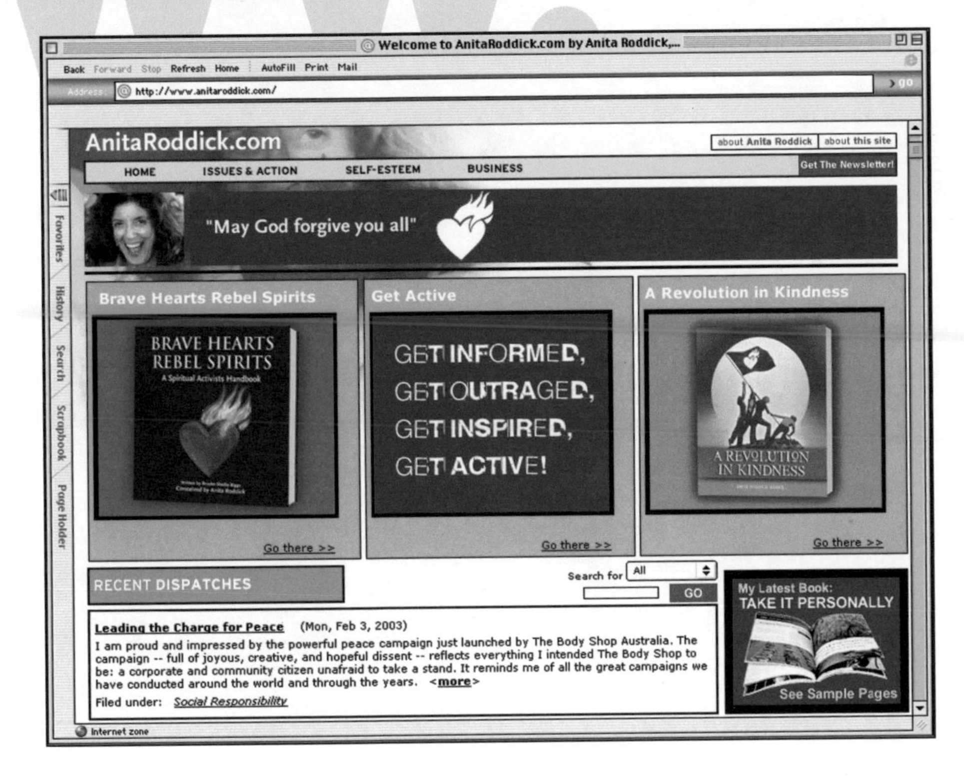

The UN estimates that in less than 25 years, if present water consumption trends continue, 5 billion people will be living in areas where it will be impossible or difficult to meet basic water needs for sanitation, cooking and drinking.